Sales is my Passion

Sales management best practices on preparation, negotiation, and closing deals with confidence

Amaro Araujo

International Key Account Manager

Copyright © 2018 Amaro Araujo

All rights reserved.

No part of this book may be reproduced in any written, electronic, recording, or photocopying without written permission of the publisher or author. The exception would be in the case of brief quotations embodied in the critical articles or reviews and pages where permission is specifically granted by the publisher or author.

ISBN-10: 1977597033
ISBN-13: 978-1977597038

DEDICATION

We're the sum of the experiences, interactions, and exchanges we have had in our lives. Learning is an everyday exercise as long as we're open to it. As I'll be talking specifically about sales management and negotiations, I want first of all to thank all the customers I've handled during the last 25 years, all the purchasers, particularly those who gave me a "hard time" they're the ones who made me improve, develop and grow in this field of cooperation, long-term relationship, and sustainable business. I want to thank colleagues with whom I have interacted and learn from, coaches and mentors, trainers and managers. All played a role – whether they know it or not – and they are far too many to list their names here, but be sure I have every one of you very present in my heart and mind and I'm deeply grateful for the time we spent together.

CONTENTS

Dedication iii

Acknowledgments vi

How to get the best out of this book vii

PART I - The Science 1

   1 - The B2B Sales World 2

   2 - You're A Natural Born Negotiator, Whether
   You Know It Or Not 12

   3 - Basic Skills Of A Sales Executive 17

   4 - The Attitudes And Behaviours 31

   5 - Know Your Market 36

   6 - Who's The Buyer? 40

PART II - The Deal Making Process 46

   6 - Preparation For A Meeting Or Negotiation 47

   7 - The Meeting: How To Lead It 53

   8 - The Offer 59

   9 - The Follow Up 67

PART III - The Practicality 71

   10 - Most Relevant Tools, Systems Or Tasks 72

11 - Sales Executive First Months PLAN 83

12 - MOST COMMON Sales Clichés 87

13 - Frequently ASKED Questions:..95

Support Material 123

About The Author.. 124

ACKNOWLEDGMENTS

There's a study showing that 90% of people would like to write a book but only some 2% actually do it. From those who actually start, a big percentage don't finish it, and an astonishing 80% that finish, don't ever get published. Reasons are more than a lot – doubt, fear (not good, failure, rejection, disappointment, reputation), uncertainty, overthinking, you name it. Therefore this book is dedicated to a couple of people, most of them virtual mentors, people I follow, read or listen on a regular basis that inspired and motivated me to move from an idea or a mere wish to this finished book you have in your hands, overcoming all those obstacles. As one of them says, "The obstacle is the way".

HOW TO GET THE BEST OUT OF THIS BOOK

This book is an A to Z guide to the sales process and will provide you with a solid foundation to help you become an expert sales executive and master the art of closing deals.

Sales isn't a "buy the book" process, but this book will provide you with the insights, knowledge, skills, attitudes, and behaviors that will make all the difference in your life in sales.

It's divided into three parts: the science, the deal-making process, and the practicality.

At the end of each topic, there's a short summary or bullet points. It's a kind of "quick reference kit" that you can consult at any time for a practical application or implementation.

PART I

The Science

In this section I set the scene so to speak, laying down the background and fundamentals of the B2B sales world and what you need to cover before stepping "into the field".

1

The B2B Sales World

There are studies showing that the sales role is one of the best-paid and rewarded in the corporate world, and the modern image of the salesperson is of someone who is extremely trustworthy, knowledgeable and skilled, therefore it is no surprise that often he or she becomes part of the Board or even makes it to CEO.

Commerce and the exchange of goods and services have been the basis of mankind's evolution, and keep growing exponentially. Each day there are new items available and we keep creating more needs. The sales role is crucial to keep the machine running and the recent growth of technology in the sales process will not reverse that but leverage it to a different level and demand of skill sets.

Despite all that evidence, there's a general feeling that sales is a very complex activity. That it requires the use of tricks and persuasion techniques perceived as negative and creates some kind of doubtful look on those on the outside. A sort of doubt between admiration and suspicion.

This book will shed light on the role and activity of the salesperson and hopefully, encourage you to step into this journey.

Sales isn't about tricks and isn't for sure about a magic formula that you can use to close deals and beat targets. If you want to become a professional in sales and make it your career and passion, be aware that there are no shortcuts. There are no "step by step" guides. It will be a journey – a step by step journey, for sure, but not step by step guide in itself, as every situation, every customer, every deal, will have its own specifics.

The profession of sales manager has evolved a lot, particularly in the last decades. There has been a kind of upgrade of the sales professionals to keep up with marketing evolution, economic growth, fierce competition and a higher level of expertise needed in their domains. Facts, studies, and details overruled simple talk, price, and persuasion.

Access to bigger markets, globalization, technology, faster and additional information, and the explosion of social media forced the sales professionals to uplift their skills and ways of working. Technology is seen as a major threat to field salespeople, but be aware of the nature of selling: people and needs (or wants, but that's another story). Someone who has something to sell and someone who's looking for that same item or solution backed up by information, expertise, outlook, advice, features, market knowledge and often times a strategic partner to assure a smooth transaction. That's where the sales professional steps in.

You might think technology and new platforms allow buying/selling without field-based salespeople. That's a peculiarity mainly of the B2C world. Nowadays you can buy items without knowing who's on the other side. You go to the internet, you order it and it gets delivered. But that's mainly for items that are not so costly or the vendor is so well known that you trust him.

Otherwise, even in the B2C (Business to Consumer) world, when we buy some expensive item (car, house, etc) we like to see the seller, you want to have a conversation, you want to understand the market. In the B2B world, that interaction and liaison between offer and demand become more important and even crucial – again, at least for relevant items- despite the easiness of e-commerce tools also available at the B2B level. A company might order non-strategic and non-expensive items without the help of a sales rep, but would they do it with an important and expensive product?

This book is mainly intended for people who are or will be dealing with B2B (Business to Business) sales. Very likely, some of the attitudes or behaviors you'll find here can be applied also to B2C (Business to Consumer) sales, but each has different requirements in terms of approach, strategy, and preparation, due to their nature.

A typical car seller dealing with private end-users has a completely different methodology than a sales manager dealing with top 500 clients. A private person goes to a dealer to buy a new car once in let's say, four, seven or ten years. Most B2B companies buy their products on a daily, weekly or monthly basis. For instance, that same car dealer selling cars to a company that has a fleet to manage would require a different approach.

To those who still have doubts or difficulties affirming themselves as salespeople or still have some thoughts of resistance, you need to recall the purpose of the function and the contribution it gives to the society. You're helping to provide or make available products and services to companies who need them to thrive and exist. Supporting them – and their co-workers – to have access to materials or solutions so they can contribute to the rest of the chain until it reaches the end user, the individuals like you and me.

A sales professional is the vehicle, the bridge between companies – sometimes from different corners of the world. It's a major contribution to an individual's comfort and quality of life in general. It would be useless to create or discover something if it would remain limited to a certain place, area or region. Salespeople are at the heart of that. Facilitating solutions, comfort, joy, health, knowledge, vision or pleasure.

You need to embed that thought in your heart and mind and treat the profession not only as a source of income but as something really useful where you can make a difference and contribute to society through your job.

The role of a sales manager has evolved a lot in the last decades. Boosted by technology and IT, but also forced to raise the bar by a more challenging market environment and far better-equipped customers. There has also been a need to redefine or reorganize the company structure and department, bringing more clarity in functions and roles that used to be a bit confusing. For instance, marketing vs sales and the link of those with R&D.

In the past, the role of a sales manager (as well as his counterpart, the buyer) was seen as a dead end or the end of a career. Folks that had joined sales would remain there for their entire life. Often times when companies didn't know what to do with someone they would offer him those positions. Sales was a routine dead-end position waiting for retirement.

But as said, corporations evolved a lot on the last decades – mostly forced by the pressure of the market and rising competition – that it came to light that those roles or departments were crucial in the company's position and ambition. Sales wasn't just an ongoing and routine exercise. Sales was the company output and ultimate source of income. It had to be leveraged and re-invented, it had to be uplifted as if the company's existence and future expansion depended on it. No more time for trivial sales techniques – sales needed to be taken seriously.

The trigger was in large part due to growing competition, but also the huge difficulty in handling objections and rejections raised by better and better-prepared purchasers. Purchasers actually did start this "renewal" process by their activity.

Companies needed to improve their results. Selling at higher margins is one side of the balance but also there, you have limits and competition. So you turn to the other side: reducing costs. Where would you start on that journey? In the purchasing department, of course. Buy cheaper, make better deals, and become smarter than the seller. Put the seller under pressure. Let's challenge the sellers, let's challenge their positions, strategies and positions, and the market. Let's promote competition among our suppliers.

In fact, while sellers were still a bit on "auto-pilot", purchasers have been the first to "wake up" from their sleep and started using new processes, technologies and sharing information. They became more professional, more organized and better prepared to object to sellers positions. Salespeople had a tough time to cope and to get through with their deals as easily as they used to. They had to do something. The time for amateurs was gone. Selling was becoming much more than offering a product and providing a price. Game over. Re-invent selling. Create professionals and experts, not messengers or vendors.

Sales departments reacted and created new frameworks and methodologies using different tools and attitudes, and revising their (almost non-existing) programs. In the end, both sellers and purchasers elevated their profession to a completely new level, where not just any employee would be able to do the job but only people with a good set of skills, attitude, behavior, and knowledge would be moving into such crucial areas.

Buying and selling became a key component in every corporation. It's not only about product and price, but market knowledge, product knowledge, innovation, solutions, different pricing methods, customer approach per their needs and requirements, instead of a one-fits-all attitude.

Fast forward. Nowadays the sales or purchasing departments are seen as the core departments of any business and are actually very coveted positions due to their status. To a point that in most companies, they are as almost a mandatory step if you want to pursue a high-level career. Often employees are stuck or blocked because of their lack of sales or customer interaction experience in their records in order to move up the corporate ladder.

Times for the "I can sell you anything" folk or the "big mouth" that could sell a fridge to an Eskimo are over. Being a sales manager is almost a science. Not a complex one, but one requiring a certain set of skills, knowledge, attitude, and behavior, making it a very complete "package". And that's what this book is about. Not a theory or a step-by-step guide, but an overview of all that it takes to thrive in the corporate sales world, directly from someone who has been there.

This book intends to demystify the role, as there are still many wrong ideas and conceptions about the sales role, and to expose how it works in real life. You won't find a lot of complex tools, jargon or systems, but I'll emmerse you in what it requires in terms of mindset and where your real contribution and difference comes from. It won't come from the tools or systems but from yourself.

During my extensive sales experience, I've seen colleagues and newcomers struggling in many situations. I struggled myself in the early days. I still remember when I had to face my first customers – big companies in the stock exchange – often doubting I could be at "their level" and able to stay steady or just giving away everything they wanted. Almost frightened, as often times, the numbers involved were huge. When you're in the early days with a small salary and you need to handle six-figure deals, it can be scary.

There are quite a few things to learn or be aware of if you want to step into the field and do a good sales job. You must acquire knowledge and skills. But being a Sales manager requires something that often times you can't learn or acquire as a process, in books or classrooms. It requires attitudes, behaviors, persuasion, and empathy. Many may say those are natural attributes – you either have them or not. My opinion is, we all have them, we just need to bring them up by awareness, discipline and supervised consistent practice. Why supervised? Because you need a mentor, a coach or someone who can guide, advise and alert you to any derailing. The risk of consistent practice without supervision is that you might be practicing in the wrong direction or in the wrong way. Practicing alone will just keep you further away from your objective.

When you have those, you have the most elementary requirements. In the next chapters, I'll go through those attitudes and behaviors and why they make a difference. I'll share the tools, systems, processes, and steps that I adopt in my daily life as a salesperson to beat my targets, build long-term relationships and close complex deals. All of it out of many years of experience, seminars, training, and of course, meeting and negotiating with all kind of customers and companies. The lost deals, the much-longer-than-expected negotiations, the giveaway or loss of customers, the closing of an unexpected deal. The real life of a salesperson with no BS. I've come to realize how much empathy plays a role in this world. Anyone can offer prices and products. Not everyone can do it with empathy. As in the famous quote, "Aim for the heart, not the head". You don't change someone's opinion using a rational argument; people make decisions emotionally, and then they use reason and facts to sustain their emotional decision, to rationalize it. So it's an emotion/reason process. And don't forget, it's much easier to convince someone with his own opinions than with yours.

Sales are about people. I'm sure I will repeat that often in this book.

My biggest deal or contract was worth $45,000,000 a year. My smallest one? Probably around $30,000. Of course, each required different time investment, resources, and work, but to both, I showed genuine interest in people, in solving their problem or providing a product they needed. I'm open, sincere, and respectful – regardless of their size. Remember, most of today's big companies were once small. Respect, regardless of the size of the company, is another attribute. But make no mistake, respect doesn't mean give them everything for free. It's all about a good balance between time, investment, and returns.

My intention in sharing the above numbers is just to make it very clear that if you're able to make a small deal, you can make a bigger one. Don't get confused by numbers or don't let numbers impress you. Depending on the market and industry, big numbers don't relate to the difficulty of the deal. There are industries that float on low figures but have very high margins and on the other side, for instance, you have the commodity businesses where the numbers involved in any transaction are of several thousands of dollars but probably with much thinner margins.

Put away the idea that company size or numbers are intrinsically related to sales complexity or with sales skills and ability. The type of organizations – and the set-up of purchasing departments – will have an impact on the way you deal with them. But not the numbers per se.

Sometimes it's much more difficult to sell a one-off or a small spot deal than to land a big contract. There's a lot more competition and limiting factors in spot deals than with big contracts, where in several areas you can make a difference (and not only the price/availability of the product).

One of the biggest obstacles and unnecessary difficulties in life is complexity. Our life is flooded with complexity and details. Don't try to complicate what is simple and don't get the idea that if it's simple it's not valuable. Make it simple. Always strive for simplicity. Any fool can make things complicated – the difficulty is in doing something simple.

This is absolutely key in sales. You don't need to add complicated formulas or elaborated pitch when something much simpler and straightforward would have brought better and quicker results.

Don't fall into the trap that you need to use jargon and sound pompous. It will have the reverse effect. If you can't say or explain something in plain English, it means you don't fully understand the topic, and the purchaser will perceive that you're trying to color something that is simply black and white.

You will fail. Be prepared for that. And it will be the best thing that could happen to you. But only if you're humble enough to seek feedback, to ask the customer why your offer wasn't accepted, and to recognize where you could have done or said something more impactful.

Life in sales isn't like the games we play at business school. It hurts when we fail out there in the real world. But use those lost deals and opportunities to stand up and improve the next negotiation. As Richard Branson said, "Business opportunities are like trains, there's always another one coming."

Every time I leave a negotiation or meeting and I have the honest feeling it didn't go that well, I don't beat up on myself. Instead, I tell myself, "Bring on the next one, it will be better." Beating up on yourself won't help. Though, recognizing weaknesses and gaps is crucial to make that "next one" better. Don't beat up on yourself, but don't put your head in the sand either, pretending all is well. Remember, there's always a place for improvement, even when you think you've "got it".

You must always be watchful and an observer of yourself, and. Take nothing for granted. Even long-lasting relationships. You have to act always as if the deal, negotiation or opportunity is at risk.

Often we have those "old" customers or loyal ones where we think things will go almost automatically or they will buy because that's what they've been doing. Stop and change that assumption immediately. Environments change, competition changes, pressure on the customer side changes, strategies change, disruption appears, purchasers are replaced.

Always run your sales without assumptions. Treat your old customers very attentively. Did their needs change? Are they going through any reorganization? Acquisition? Are the premises of their purchasing department the usual ones? Is competition at the door?

Don't lay back. Don't ever lay back. Competition is watching you. One false step and your loyal customer goes away – and it's not his fault. It's your fault, for being distracted and taking things for granted.

Main Message Wrap-Up:

- You will fail. Be ready for that. Be attentive and watchful. Debrief and understand what you can do better in the next round.

- Sales isn't about tricks and exploring weaknesses in people but in building trust and long-term relationships, seizing opportunities, and coming across as a trustworthy expert in your field.

- Don't fall into the trap that you need to use jargon, clutter and sound pompous. Avoid complexity.

- Don't assume big numbers mean more complex negotiations or important sales skills. It's not about the numbers themselves, but in how relevant the items become to your customers.

- Empathy is key: Aim at the heart, not the head.
- Sales and purchasing are key departments in any company.
- Sales is not about having a textbook, even one like this. You can't become "certified" as a sales professional (well, there might be some certifications but that doesn't guarantee your ability and success).
- Nothing is for granted. Even long-lasting customer relationships. Don't ever sit back and relax. Competition is watching you – one false step and your loyal customer goes away and it's not his fault. It's your fault, for being distracted and taking things for granted.

2

You're A Natural Born Negotiator, Whether You Know It Or Not

Some people have the negative image of a salesperson or the sales role, as people who use tricks and manipulation to fool the others. This is due to a certain cliché or the image of an aggressive salesperson or selling behavior. Take for instance the example of door-to-door, telesales or car salespeople. But that's mainly in B2C. Though to the common citizen, sales is sales, they don't really get the picture of the difference between B2C and B2B.

B2B sales have nothing to do with it. You're pushy or you use tricks once, not twice. B2B foundations are built on trust, knowledge, expertise, loyalty, perseverance, and patience. There is no place for tricks. You aren't being pushy here, but you can face – and you will – face a pushy purchaser. It's up to you how to deal with him.

Many other people admire the role of a salesperson but think they don't have what it takes, or feel they don't know the tricks or have the "poker" face to do the job. They think they're too nice or not equipped to overcome a negotiation. So they wonder and they doubt if they could do a sales role.

Guess what, you're negotiating every single day. All of us are. From the moment you wake up until the moment you go to sleep. From your childhood until your elderly days.

- You negotiate with your parents: why you can't go out with your friends or on a road trip.

- You negotiate with your friends: which bar you guys should go to tonight, and who's driving.

- You negotiate with your girlfriend: to watch football or "Friends" on TV.

- You negotiate with your siblings: who's cleaning the bathroom or takes the dog out.

- You negotiate with your wife: if you're going to her parents or to your friend's for dinner.

- You negotiate with your teachers: if you have to finish your project this week or within a few additional days.

- You negotiate with your boss: your holidays and even your performance appraisal.

Guess what, you negotiate even with yourself. Almost every moment of the day:

- The moment the alarm rings you wonder, "Should I get up now or stay more five minutes in bed?"

- Should I go for a hamburger or salad?

- Should I drink one more beer or have I had enough?

- Should I ask her to marry me or not?

- Should I do as they say or do it my own way?

- Should I buy a house or rent it?

- Should I apply for that role or wait for a better opportunity?

- Should I dress casual or formal?

- What do I do now?

  (Questions like this will show you negotiating using both emotions and reason. And there's the difficulty – the conflict between both – that paralyzes you. So you negotiate with yourself and then you try to reason why this is the best way to go. Yes, we need to be consistent with our decisions and back them up.)

Every single day, whether you want to or not, whether you know it or not, you're negotiating. The question is, how good are you at that? How often are you able to get the what you expected? Are you happy with the success rate of your negotiations? Are you just letting go to not start a discussion (negotiation)? Do you avoid confrontation? Or do you sometimes let go and sometimes you fight for your idea? It's all about negotiation, mediation, finding common ground, some concessions, some trades. Right? What do you think selling in the B2B world is?

Even in your own personal life, you're a negotiator (or label it as you want). Now, put that to good use and start a job in sales and take it to the next level.

It's all about consistent practice, watching what works and what doesn't. Learning, observing, listening and getting prepared to face those who are equipped on their end to challenge you.

I need to underline one aspect that alongside persuasion, influence and your capacity to articulate your position, there is another important factor that can unbalance the negotiation process and play an important role in the outcome: (ab)use of position and strength. As in your personal life, this will also happen in the B2B negotiations.

In some cases due to the particular relationship of the participants involved, one side might use their position to impose their "rules" or to weight the arguments with completely different scales. A dispute or negotiation between parents/kids or managers/employees are good examples that can, and in most cases will be influenced by a "power position". The same can happen in business. Bigger customers will use it shamelessly. Medium customers will try to play in the big guy's playground as well. But also you – depending on your position as a supplier – may use this "power play" across your portfolio.

Pick your battles. Choose which ones are worth fighting for or not. Remember, we have a limited social capital, don't waste it with minor things, regardless of which position you're in.

Maybe you've never looked at it as a negotiation as it is something that has been there since your early existence, with one exception: when you were a new-born and a few months/years old. You could get away with it. You could get almost anything you wanted when you were a baby, unable to talk or express yourself in common language.

When you've learned to talk, negotiation jumped in. Remember your parents: "Eat this and I'll give you that." Remember those fights in the supermarket "I want that toy", or at the restaurant "I don't want soup"? Call it discussion, diplomacy or dispute. It was all about negotiating. You've negotiated since a very young age, and you won't stop until you die. So make good use of your daily experience to improve your negotiation skills.

As they will be needed throughout your life, they will be critical in the corporate world, not only at the sales level but overall in your career. Don't you think you'll have to negotiate your next position? Your salary? Your car? Your bonus? Your performance? This will happen all the way up (or down) in the corporate world, whether you have a sales role or not. Thing is, sales folks should get away as winners on those confrontations, it's their field.

But again, being properly aware and equipped will help you to be more empathic, a good listener, patient, focused on solutions and positions instead of people. Putting your ego aside, you'll grow your competency and ability to prepare, negotiate and close win/win deals with less struggle and far more pleasure. You'll become a proud sales manager.

Main message Wrap up:

- When you've learned to talk, you learned the art of negotiation.

- You're negotiating every single day with those around you. All of us are. From the moment you wake up until the moment you go to sleep. Negotiate with friends, parents, colleagues or bosses

- It's all about mediation, finding common ground, some concessions, some trades. Right? Even in your own personal life. With your wife, parents or kids. So you're a negotiator (or label it as you want).

- You negotiate even with yourself. Almost every moment of the day. Should I do this or not? Go this or that way? Eat fish or meat? It's all a matter of persuasion, convincing, having what the other party wants or needs (in many cases, yourself).

- Often, negotiation is a power play. Customers play with the size of their company, reputation or position. They will ask for more, they think they can have more. In sales, you can be on one side or the other. Just be aware of this, and don't let it hinder your preparation and expected outcomes.

3

Basic Skills Of A Sales Executive

The role of the Sales Manager is seen as entrepreneurial, independent and senior. It doesn't mean you can't find young people in the role, in fact, you'll see them more and more. Just look at how business schools and studies are getting popular and coveted that's a clear sign of the relevance of the role. In this matter, seniority isn't properly linked to the age of the person but the experience on the job.

The old image (again, old images haunt this role) that the sales manager is a fat guy in his 50's, wearing a large suit, and carrying a big briefcase is gone. As previously explained, the role of the sales manager has evolved a lot in the last decades and with this, its image.

A modern B2B sales manager is somewhere in his or her late 20's (we gained one or two generations in the last couple of years), educated, often with a college degree, fit, with good appearance and image, mastering new technologies and tools, a fine talker, smart dresser, and carrying a laptop or mobile. Superconnected, updated with what's happening in the market, and often driving a company car.

In this section, I want to highlight some of the attitudes, behaviors, and skills a sales manager needs to have or is expected to master when stepping into this role (or is expected to have in short time, in case he's just starting his career). Do you need to have them all? To a certain extent yes, or at least the more you have, the easier it makes your life. If you feel you're short on any, develop, learn, read, observe and practice them. Consistent practice with necessary corrections will lead you there. I have an particular emphasis in two areas – productivity and time management – as those will be mainly responsible for your good balance.

- **Relationship-building capacity:** When I'm asked at any social event what my job is or what I do, I tend to say that my role is an account manager, but I don't sell anything – I manage relationships with customers. This is exactly how I feel about it. Not selling, not pushing to reach targets, not fooling customers. Managing. Helping to move product A that my company produces to company B who needs that product, by means of a relationship with my counterpart. Based on trust, respect, vision, understanding, and acceptance. Often times there's negotiation, that is a question of bridging their aims with our expectations.

- **Work Independently:** This will depend a lot on what kind of manager you have. The standard model presumes that the sales manager is a responsible individual, and gives you the freedom to manage your portfolio, region, work and goal tracking. To be a problem solver and to have initiative. With regular updates on your goals vs objectives. Unfortunately, there are also managers that have very strict and "micromanagement" behavior. This is very frustrating and limiting to a sales manager, and at the same time is a challenge of your resilience and capacity to deal with adversity. Most sales directors will tell you, "Come to me for forgiveness, don't come for permission." Don't expect people to tell you what to do, you must be "hands on the job".

- **Be disciplined:** In most cases, you'll be home-based or traveling alone. You'll be on your own. Discipline is very important to keep your balance, to finish your tasks on time and to keep you sharp. One of a home-based or field sales manager's major challenges is the work life/balance. Have the discipline to separate your personal life from your professional one. This can be challenging at the beginning, as very often people fall into the trap of the "fusion". Always available for business and always available for the family; when in reality, they're never at 100% on one side or the other. There's no rule without exception, but as much as possible, create your boundaries for the good of the business and your familiar entourage. The same applies to traveling. Keep a good balance and don't use the excuse of work duties to be always traveling. Remember, you can always find another job but family is something that if you drop it, it's gone. And if that happens, it will affect your work performance. So the work/life balance isn't just propaganda, it's a requirement for good performance (on both sides).

- **Efficiency:** A sales manager is often traveling and on the road. This means less time to follow up emails and pending actions. Therefore you need to have efficient systems and processes to help you out. Cut or reduce any task that doesn't have any added value. Delegate. Ask for help – that's not a sign of weakness but of courage. Don't get involved in things that don't matter. Ask people to not copy you in useless emails, answer emails at the end of the day, emails aren't urgent. Any urgency should be a call, not an email.

- **Organization:** Again, when mastering a role that requires discipline, independence, and initiative, you will need to be well organized in order to have quick access to information, archives, and never miss a meeting, important call or deadline. Organize your email and folders to get clear and fast access to what's relevant. Organize yourself in such a way that you know what's expected or scheduled for the next day or the current week. Prepare. Think ahead. Plan. Organize. Don't let fortune (or misfortune) get in the way. You're a professional, not an amateur.

- **Productivity**: We're always too busy. I remember a period when I felt I was losing control of the situation (workload). The solution I found was working longer and longer in the foolish hope I would catch up with the backlog. Getting more things done would bring the situation back to normal. Wishful thinking. When you don't change habits and ways of working, working longer will only increase the number of inefficient tasks. It's useless to work a lot or longer if you're working on trivial things. Below you may find some of my learning out of that experience.

1. Plan your day ahead if possible the previous evening. Having that plan in your subconscious will set up the mood in your brain and you'll know where and when to focus when you're about to start your day.

2. Don't jump between tasks, otherwise, you'll have to catch up with the rhythm again and you'll have the feeling nothing is finished (and it isn't). Focus on one task, finish it, then move on to your daily target list.

3. Take breaks. Every hour take a small walk (to the coffee machine, for instance). Breathe fresh air if possible; your brain needs oxygen to think. Don't take this as a waste of time, it can refill and refresh your mind/ideas.

4. Thank people for helping or supporting you, or thank them for whatever other reason. Being grateful releases happiness and optimism and that supports creativity and clarity.

5. Say no. Saying yes to all kind of requests from colleagues or managers won't improve your quality of work. You need to know your limits and your limitations. Say no whenever you're in doubt if you'll meet a deadline or if you will be able to present valuable content.

6. Be proactive instead of reactive. If you want to avoid being driven by tasks and by the agenda of others or colleagues. Be proactive. Anticipate. Finish tasks before the deadline so people don't chase you. Provide info before people come to you. Communicate clearly so people don't ask you for explanations. Make more use of telephone and face to face meetings rather than emails.

7. Don't let emails drive your day. When it's really urgent, people will call you. Check emails three or four times a day (morning, after lunch, mid-afternoon).

8. Social media. A complete time killer if you don't step back. Like your email, establish routines to look at your smartphone. Establish that goal and track the progress. You'll see how hard it is, but you'll also notice that keeping away provides you more focus and time to do what really matters.

9. You can't be everywhere and on top of everything. Trust and empower people. Colleagues who feel empowered normally over-deliver. This way you can free up time to focus on other things, on the bigger picture.

10. Deliver through others. Use the skills, knowledge, and the experience of colleagues and peers to achieve your milestones.

Don't trade time with your friends or loved ones to do tasks that have no added value or are simply bad habits. Change habits, get the work done and shut down the business mode on time.

- **Have some knowledge of the OTC (Order to Cash) process:** Even if you have a "customer Service center" or inside sales team to handle and take care of the orders until they are delivered and cashed in, it's good to know or understand what happens behind the scenes, as once in a while there will be challenges (order not registered, delayed, invoice not being paid and therefore overdue). I won't go into much detail on this but take some time to speak with people handling that process so you're not caught completely off guard when a customer brings this issue to a discussion.

- **Time management:** In order to become independent, productive, efficient and organized, you need to manage your time properly. If you don't manage time, you'll be managed by time. You'll be running through your agenda items and doing what people need instead of what you need to do. Time is one of your most important limited resources. It won't stretch, it won't come back, and it won't be better tomorrow. As most of the time you'll be on your own – at home, in the office or traveling – you'll need to set your priorities right and focus on what has to be done, what must be done, what can be delegated or what won't be done at all. You'll have to be in the driving seat. Remember, you're in a role/position that requires decision making.

These are some considerations about Time management:

The famous Eisenhower method

	Urgent	Not Urgent
Important	Crying baby Kitchen fire Some calls 1	Exercise Vocation Planning 2
Not Important	3 Interruptions Distractions Other calls	4 Trivia Busy work Time wasters

Source: Wikipedia By Rorybowman (Own work) [Public domain], via Wikimedia Commons

Where tasks should classify under a 4-box matrix: Not important / Important / Urgent / Not urgent. I have to admit this had a very positive impact on the way I was working a couple of years ago. But I wasn't using it the right way. In my head, I did the ranking as:

1-Urgent and important   2-Important

                            Not urgent

3-Urgent, not important   4-Not important

                            Not urgent

That's quite OK, but there's another way to push it to the next level:

The box **4 not urgent not important**: Why should you care to waste time with these tasks? Simply put them out of your way. No brainer. Say no, delegate.

The box **3 Urgent not important**: Why should you allocate time and resources to something that doesn't bring any added value? Not important? Out with it.

Ok, we just have two left. Now you face a dilemma. Imagine you have only sufficient time to allocate to one box. Which one would it be?

Probably you'd pick the box **1 Urgent and important**. These are the fires that need to be extinguished right away. Ok, let's pick that one and extinguish those fires.

What happens the next day? You bet. The tasks you had on **box 2 Important not urgent** became urgent and are now in box one. And while they moved to **box 1**, new ones came to **box 2**. So you keep on turning the wheel like a hamster focusing your day on **box 1** because it will be full every single day with tasks and activities coming from **box 2**.

If you put your focus on **box 2 Important not urgent**, you actually prevent the fires from starting and remove yourself from being a fireman day in, day out. The secret of excellence in time management is focusing on **box 2**. Of course, at the beginning, this demands effort and some sacrifice, but in the long run, it means you have your priorities under control and you know exactly where to focus and dedicate your time without running left to right, and ultimately lead you to lose that feeling of being overloaded. You allocate your energy and focus on the right tasks and priorities, creating space to understand what you're doing and mastering your day. Focusing on **box 2** will gradually extinguish **box 1**.

- There's nothing more useless than doing something outstanding that shouldn't be done at all.

- **Reporting/Handling systems:** Whether you like it or not, reporting and filing systems will be part of your duties and regular activities, so be prepared and schedule time for them.

Don't let it get to a point where you're chased by your manager or supervisors who send you gentle reminders of a deadline not met or reports not updated. This is a waste of time – of your time and of other people's time (remember productivity, efficiency, discipline, time management?. It just leads to more frustration and negative energy. If we're talking about agreed tasks and timelines, do them on the schedule. If it's not possible, inform them upfront. But don't come after the due date with opinions like, "This is nonsense, it's a useless tool or report". There's a time and place to have that discussion before you agree to it. Once agreed, deliver. As simple as that. Never over-promise, ever over-deliver.

- **Persuasive skills:** One of the key characteristic of a sales manager. Don't confuse this with tricks or the capacity to abuse people's weaknesses. There are some well-known ways to influence people to buy:
    - Large request/small request (you ask a higher price, then make a revision and offer a substantial small. Customers will have the feeling you did a big step towards their direction when in the end the price is still too high).
    - Social proof (when you use your market share position, branding or reputation in your discussions)
    - Established authority (when some authority in the segment backs up your product)
    - Use of reciprocation (when you did a discount previously and expects the customer to "pay" that back accepting your current price or increasing orders)
    - Feeling of scarcity (when you let know the product might go out of stock)
    - Connotation (when you lead the customer to assume or link your product with something he holds as positive

or impactful – but it's a mere perception)

There obviously many others, for more in-depth details and understanding I'd strongly recommend *Influence*, a book by Robert Cialdini.

Aside from those "techniques", there's also your own personality. Your capacity to listen and explain, understand and support, ability to expose, and sustain your positions.

At this point, it would also be very interesting and important to know why customers buy from you. Is it because:

- They trust you?
- You've connected and build foundations for a long-term relationship?
- You manage to cover perfectly the wants/needs of your customer?
- Is your offer really competitive?
- Does your customer see value beyond and above your price?
- Is your company is a market reference for them?
- Do they perceive you to be an expert?
- They just need another supplier to divide the risk/credit/alternatives?

You might have one or several reasons, but I'd strongly recommend you to find out (and not assume) why customers buy from you in order to explore those strengths further and to improve areas you might not have noticed.

We can include here the so-called KLT factor: Know, like, trust. People who actually know you, like you and trust you are very inclined to do business with you.

- **Planning:** Remember the old quote "Failing to prepare is preparing to fail.". You need to coordinate visits, budgets, and sales plan. You need to prepare for your customer visits and negotiation sessions. Often you have to bring your management and the customer's management to the meeting. Don't look like an amateur during that process, it will weaken your position and image. When planning a customer visit, send the agenda points ahead of time and ask the customer if he has any other points to add. Ask him if anyone else will be joining. Work professionally. Be a professional, a reference.

- **Personal and professional development:** This is a fast-changing world. Don't rely on your existing skills or achievements. Remember, one of your major strengths is your role as an expert and as an authority in your field. Don't accept the status quo. Develop your strengths further and work on your weaknesses. Have plans for your personal and professional development. Together with your employer or alone. In the end, it's your responsibility, as it's your life and passion we're talking about. There's an endless source of resources available. No excuses. No time? Then you need to work on your planning and time management. Don't expect that this is a company task. It's also your task to ensure it's an ongoing process.

- **Have the long-term in mind:** B2B business is based on trust and mutual respect offering and sourcing competitive solutions and innovations. Normally people stay in these roles for quite a while. It takes time to build a relationship. It takes time to nurture it and explore its full potential. Eventually, there comes a time to leave or separate, but the mutual feeling of respect and appreciation will remain. Don't just have in mind what you can earn this year, but what you can benefit in the mid/long run. Shortcomings are not the foundations of your business and role. Shortcomings are short benefits. Sometimes you need them. Question improving cash position, gain a one-off deal. But those are side gains and good to have, but the real must-have is in the long run. Sales management is a marathon, an endurance race, not a sprint. And as in other areas of your life, we can adopt the motto "If you want to go fast, go alone. If you want to go far, go together". And going together means with your customer and with your internal stakeholders. You can't make it on your own.

- **The capacity of good rationale:** You're probably have heard about the "sell me this pen" question? Often times presented as the standard to see a salesperson's capacity.

- There are a couple of urban myths like this one, giving the idea that we can see the caliber of a salesperson and their ability according to this answer. The usage of that question might have worked in the past, though and nowadays HR and hiring managers are not looking for "the right" answer, as indeed there isn't one, but the logic and the argument used to justify a certain position or approach. You can find all kind of examples if you make a quick search on the internet, some very funny, some seemingly very "wise" and aggressive. My question is, why would you sell one pen if you could sell a full bucket of them or refill a customer's pen needs every month? Think broader, think long term. You could eventually make one good sale and earn a huge margin with one item. But would that make you a great sales guy? Always have this in mind: it doesn't start with what you want or need, it starts with what the customer wants or needs. What would have more value, to make a one-time sale of an expensive fridge to an Eskimo – he would find out very soon he was misled by you – or to be patient and sell him a heater fuelled by gas and refilling it every six months? Yes, it's more logical, therefore you'd face more competition, but you wouldn't be selling something people would not need or use at all and your chances to sell a second item would be down to zero.

- **Are you a "hunter" or a "farmer":** Each salesperson has his own personality and ambitions. Of course, there are certain common denominators to all – respect for the customers and profession, ethics, target-driven and solution-focused – but let's face it, we're all different and we all meet those standards by taking different paths. The mix of the basic ingredients is different from person to person. No right or wrong. For example:

- o **The hunters**: These are sales folks eager to go and close a deal. To go and find new customers or markets. To play it a bit hard and to the point. They're pretty much results-driven and less patient on long-term projects. They get a bit annoyed that it might represent the investment of a year to get a client on board. They go and "kill". They grab their prey, they bring it "home" and off they go again.

- o **The farmers**: These are the "patient" sales folks. They base their work and results on the long-term investment and vision. They're not at ease with "go and close a deal quickly". They nurture their customers and they collect the results in a sustainable and long-term manner. They explore customer's full potential, instead of grabbing just the visible part. They're conscious of the fact that the market is difficult and loyalty is a slow process but pays off.

Is there an ideal profile you should have? It will depend a lot on where your company is, and your strategy and vision for the short/mid and long term. Ideally, you should be able to adapt to both. Ideally. I don't think a "natural" farmer can be an excellent "hunter" and vice versa. But he can be a very good hybrid, doing both rather well. But it's not optimal. You can't survive if you don't have customers today, so you need to be a hunter. On the other hand, you won't have a future if you don't work on your customer pipeline nor nurture your current customers.

In the ideal world, a sales team should have both components or elements. In the ideal world, one sales manager should be both a farmer and a hunter. In my experience, having met and dealt with hundreds of salespeople, farmers will always be farmers and hunters...may one day become farmers. Why can't a farmer become a hunter? Very challenging. He would need to be "re-wired".

The best thing to do - and I believe most companies use this approach - is to balance each sales executive with a customer portfolio comprised of different kinds of customers: opportunistic, regular/loyal, strategic partners, contracts and a new business development target.

That way each individual sales team member would have to put to use both skills of farming and hunting.

But there's no single approach, and each company is a different reality. Is it better to be a hunter or a farmer? There's no right or wrong. Be a balance between both. The important thing is to know the strategy and vision of the sales department, discuss with the sales director and rest of the team members so that all resources and strengths are properly allocated in the most optimal manner. You can squeeze an orange as much as you want, all you will get is more orange juice. You'll never have apple juice out of an orange.

Main message wrap-up:

- Relationship-building capacity: Business is about people, people are driven by emotions ahead of reason.

- Able to work independently: Most of the time you'll be on your own and alone in your home office or road. You'll be like your own boss.

- Be disciplined: lack or low supervision may "soften" your discipline. Be your own supervisor.

- Efficiency: set up systems and procedures to optimize your time and results.

- Organization: together with efficiency, you need to be properly organized to keep a few balls in the air at the same time and not let them fall.

- Productivity: Companies pay for performance, not for time traveling or in the office. You won't be rewarded for that but by the results you achieve.

- Time management: Time is the scarcest resource on earth and will be your worst enemy. Master it or it will master you.

- Persuasion: No BS and no tricks. Use facts, market conditions, real solutions and value to the customer, show real interest.

- Planning: Planning is everything, the plan is nothing. You need to know where you're heading even if along the way you need to adjust the course. No stubbornness, a plan is a compass and every now and then you need to adjust course.

- Hunters Vs Farmers: What is your sales DNA like? Are you good at quickly finding and closing deals but get bored managing relationships? Or good at building and maintaining relationships and not that comfortable with prospecting or closing quick deals? Try to keep a good balance between them. Be a farmer with hunting skills.

- Have the long-term in mind: unless on very specific occasions or opportunities, forget the immediate pleasure. You can fool a customer once, you won't do it twice. Your company needs that same customer next year or for the next decade.

4

The Attitudes And Behaviours

How do you land that multimillion-dollar deal? How do you become one of those super-self-confident sales guys who doesn't shake in front of a big and powerful customer? How do you become the "best in class" of your team? You're aware of the skills and knowledge needed to succeed in this role, but is that it? Anyone nowadays can acquire skills and knowledge, so does that mean anyone can be a salesperson? Sorry, not that simple. There are a couple of things to add up and are not so easy to acquire. How do you become a top sales executive?

- By listening. As rule of thumb, during a meeting or negotiation, the sales rep should prompt the buyers to talk by asking probing and open questions. Buyers should talk 65% of the time and purchasers 35%.

- By taking action. Knowledge isn't power. Action is based on knowledge. Your knowledge is useless if it's not implemented.

- By being very watchful of yourself during any customer visit or negotiation. Be an observer of yourself.

- By not letting yourself fall into emotional or personal reactions.

- By following and watching experienced people doing a few deals and customer visits.

- By doing it yourself, again and again.

- By consistent practice, not only for the routine but with commitment.

- By asking for feedback from all your entourage.

- By losing deals (and knowing the exact reasons you did, not the reasons you think).

I strongly recommend that on your first customer visits (and also later, once in a while) you go together with a colleague. He can be an experienced sales manager, marketing manager or technical colleague. Don't feel that you're being judged or examined – consider it as giving you more confidence. Doing this allows you to:

- Feel more relaxed and at ease as there are two of you, one can always go in "support" of the other.

- Have more time to observe.

- Your colleague will probably raise questions you wouldn't think about.

- Ask him for feedback on your overall performance (body language, quality of questions, leading the discussion). This is absolutely crucial as we can't see ourselves and often we have the wrong idea of how we do things.

The best sales managers weren't born that way. They too have come a long way. It's an ongoing process. Of maturation, of learning, of closing gaps, of observing, of letting go and of losing deals.

Remember, it's all about people. Therefore, even if there are some "tricks and observations" that can help you during negotiations, there's no simple "step-by-step system" that could give you a clear advantage towards a purchaser, because there are far too many personal and emotional parameters, often not following a logical sequence. Certainly, there are a good number of tools and processes, approaches and methods that every sales manager should be aware of – and use – but don't expect that you'll become a great sales manager by your competence with processes and systems, but by your capability to "read" and interact with people. That's where the big things happen –together with the willingness to improve, to do better, to go the extra mile, to fail and keep moving forward.

Let's pick up some very outstanding examples: you surely know names like Lionel Messi, Cristiano Ronaldo, Rafael Nadal, Usain Bolt, Elon Musk, or Richard Branson. Probably you've been tempted to read their biographies, articles, and posts like "The 10 habits of X" or"How to become as successful as Z".

Nowadays anyone can have access to and acquire information, skills or knowledge. But does that means everyone will reach a top level? No? Why?

Simple. Despite the fact that all Messi's and Ronaldo's teammates have been training the same way, all have the same coach and share the same "company culture" – and have the same access to all systems and tools – they don't all reach the same level. The same applies to tennis players or business people, they're all aware of the "processes" and systems but all end up in different rankings. Even the ranking isn't taken for granted, there are shifts every now and then. Nothing is carved in stone.

The secret isn't about following a step-by-step process but in the individuals themselves. It's about how are we are "fit for purpose" in that area. The "you" specific component plays a major role. How much you want it, how much it fits your dreams and vision, how it fits within your boundaries, how much you believe it, and how much you're open, humble and ready to do it.

Habit formation, routines, and discipline all have a role to play in our lives and whatever we attempt to achieve, as well as knowledge and skills. What I want to underline is that, as in many areas of our lives, sales is about a mix of things and one important part of it is who you are vs who the purchaser is.

Processes, methods, and systems are just other pieces that will complete the puzzle.

I'm repeating this once in a while to manage your expectations. Often people – and particularly millennials –are on the lookout for magic tricksand quick schemes to reach their goals.

There aren't shortcuts if you want to embrace a long-lasting sales career. It's a big, wide-open road. Not all well paved and properly maintained. It's going to be bumpy and tricky, but it's going to be worth riding on it.

Having that in mind, the best way to get through is by showing genuine interest in individuals (or corporations as their representatives), their wants and needs.

Would selling a fridge to an Eskimo make you a greater or better salesman? No. It would certainly make you earn some bucks and the admiration of a short-sighted manager, but wouldn't serve anyone's purpose in the mid-long term.

Build and maintain relationships (both internally and with customers) in a very respectful manner.

Build customer relationships based on trust and sincerity.

Empathy is key in a sales role. Is this a natural attribute or can you leverage it? Almost everything in ourselves can be leveraged if we really want to and shift our minds that direction. Read, listen, watch and practice consistently.

Aim to have both sides happy (your company and the customer). Does it happens always? Hell no.

Does it mean if one side isn't that happy, you're not a good salesperson? Well, it depends. If you're aware and you're working on the subject, you are on the right path.

Remember, the aim of a salesperson is a "win-win" situation. And remember as well, "win-win" doesn't necessarily mean a 50/50 situation. Why do so many people get stuck with this idea? if I have a 40/60 situation am I not winning? If 40% represents even more (or at lower cost) than I expected, who cares if he goes away with 60%?

Don't look or think about customers as numbers. Customers aren't an abstract thing or a P&L. It's all about people. People who have personal lives, good and bad days, just as you do. Individuals with ambitions and setbacks, with wants and needs, with limited time available. Individuals in need of your help and support to keep their business running, and to provide them with ammunition to convince their internal stakeholders that this is a good deal. Help them out. The better your arguments are, the better use they'll make of them to convince their internal stakeholders.

Main message wrap-up:

- **Empathy:** Ability to understand and share the feelings of another.
- **Capacity to listen.** To encourage purchasers to expose their objections, their doubts, their market view.
- **Consistent Practice:** Action is key, feedback is a must, failing is part of the process.
- **Persuasion:** Action aimed to change a person's attitude or behavior.
- **Influence:** The act of producing effects on the actions, behavior or opinions of another.
- **Capacity to build trust and long-term relationships.** Technology can enable and speed up processes, but people are at the heart of anything being transmitted from A to B in the corporate world.
- **Clear communication.** Don't communicate drop by drop, send all the info at once. Don't refer to abstract comparisons (this is 10% more productive. More productive than what?

5

Know Your Market

In this chapter, I want to shed some light on a number of aspects that are crucial or expected from a sales manager, directly from the territory. One of the reasons he's an important piece of the puzzle of business-to-business sales: knowledge (product/market/trends/innovation), outlook – factual and visionary. A trusted source of information, not only a messenger but with a broader view of the market, as he has access to background information not available to his customers.

If you're in your early steps or if you didn't yet start your sales career, don't be overwhelmed by the fact that you're not familiar with your market (or even which market you should be familiar with). You'll have time and occasions to learn. Learn from existing colleagues, from reports, from internal departments. Don't pretend you know something you don't. Be honest and open. Read. Source information. Nowadays information is widely available, you just need to find out the best references so as not to lose your time with useless stuff. Market indexes, pricing indexes, industry associations – all are good sources of information and your own work in the field and experience will fill in what's missing. You'll build up that knowledge and overview along the way.

Market Landscape: The sales manager must know his market, the dynamics of the region/country and their link to a wider picture of European or interdependency of global markets. Very often, prices in Europe go up or down, not actually because of the supply/demand in this region but due to oversupply or shortage in the US or Asia. It's important to know all the market dynamics so you're able to explain fluctuations in price or feedstock or raw materials that don't seem logical.

Products/Product portfolio: Become familiar with your products or services. The different categories, applications and how they're divided by groups.

Know their background as main costs, performance, specifications, features, gaps or strength as opposed to similar competition.

If possible have a table showing the competition's "compatibility". This is important as you can immediately propose an alternative to a customer or explain the benefits of your material/service. Have the right product. Don't just propose something that can do the job.

Competition: Who are they, where are they, how do they operate, how are they present in the market, do they have any cost or competitive advantage, what are their weaknesses, what are their products and pricing strategy, what is their market share.

Newcomers: New competitors of yours or of your customers can and will disturb the market. The existent players will need to accommodate a new one and for sure this will be both a challenge but also an opportunity. If you don't want to be caught unguarded, know your enemies. Remember, the price is the last differentiator between players. Don't rush to reduce prices just to keep your market share, that's the last thing to do (or, not do).

Outlook: Don't be just a price messenger. One of your add values (and one of the reasons customers will like to talk to you or to have you visit their offices from time to time) is so that you can share what you/your company feels, sees or expects is coming. You're the "behind the scenes" man that they trust. Information is key, anticipation is crucial in business. Are prices likely to go up or down? Is there any major change in the market – is a competitor short of material? Shutdown for a maintenance? are the imports rising? Any seasonal peak? Feedstock rising? All of this put properly together is info that allows the customer to anticipate, react to or simply acknowledge.

Legislation: New legislation can disrupt markets or segments, but most of all, can create anxiety and confusion amongst your customers. Being well informed and aware is again another strength of a sales manager to play the role of the "expert". This matter can lead to changes in formulations, additional costs, replacement of raw materials. So when there are some rumors, customer rely on the knowledge and privileged position of the sales manager to keep them properly informed (often supported or led by other internal stakeholders as regulatory or compliance).

Shifts and trends in the industry: Another area where the sales manager is a vector of information with his wider or global view. Customers are always eager to know what is going in the market globally. Is it moving towards different ideas? Are there alternative products popping up?

Regional view vs local: You need to get the wider picture per your company perspective. You need to be aware that there will be different levels of attractiveness in "regions", countries or areas. Some will be core regions or countries, others will be development or target regions and some other "supportive" regions. This happens following the company's positioning in the market, presence in the market, logistics, costs, margins, and optimization. From a sales manager's perspective, dealing with "supportive" countries is obviously a bit frustrating. Most likely you'll have less support and focus on the business.

Besides having a good talk with your management on how to balance the situation, you need to think "enterprise first" and see it from a company perspective. "Supportive" regions are needed to keep the balance of the market and not oversupply the core regions, but I agree it might be more challenging to be a sales executive in a core region than in a supportive one. I've been in both.

Main message Wrap up:

- Your products and portfolio range, application, main features
- Market landscape
- Competition
- Newcomers
- Market outlook
- Legislation changes
- Shifts and trends in the industry
- Global or wider view (broader than your single market or region)

6

Who's The Buyer?

If you're familiar with the book, *The Art of War*, by Sun Tzu, you know how important it is to know your enemy, its background, strategy, ambitions, needs, weaknesses, and strengths. Although the buyer isn't an enemy, (he's ultimately an opponent who often times becomes almost a friend) you'll need the same approach or principle, to get to know the person behind the job title of purchaser or buyer.

This will give you a clear advantage. It won't solve all of your problems or challenges as they're part of the buy/sell world, but it will allow you to be ready, prepared. To anticipate, to meet his expectations, to close deals.

Don't ever neglect this step of knowing your counterpart as well as you can. Remember what I've said numerous times: it's not (only) about who you are and what you aim for. A big part of the equation concerns who he is, what drives him and what he wants. If you don't know who he really is, how can you know what he wants?

Below you will find a few critical aspects about purchasers that you should study or think about when you're preparing a regular meeting, a negotiation, a proposal or working on your leads/prospects.

Who is the buyer?

A well-trained professional with a broad business understanding is a critical part of the success of his company. Someone with targets – not only to reduce or contain costs but also quality, supply, and so on. Someone who's there in his function to challenge you as he aims for the best product/service and the best conditions. Note that I said, conditions, I didn't say price. Regardless of how good your offer is, he will very likely object or challenge you for a better deal. So keep some concessions in your pocket. He will test boundaries, as you should do as well.

Are there different buyers types?

As you have different styles of salespeople, you'll also find different styles of purchasers. Not exactly around the same labeling and fields, but very focused on their end, background and they will use all that's in their power to shake your position, so the more you know about them the better you can adjust your strategy to get them on your side, or at least more collaborative.

The Emotional: Someone who will always blame you for high prices and hold you responsible for everything that goes against his expectations. He hides his insecurity and low market knowledge with this emotional approach. Don't ever take any business discussion with him personally or to heart.

The Accountant: Listens a lot, knows the market, uses all kind of data and analysis to sustain his positions and make comparisons to put you under pressure.

The Bossy: Talks a lot, has good market knowledge, normally in the job for a long while. Uses the salesman as a source of info and will play it. He knows he's in a favorable position as he knows what your competition is saying and doing.

The Technical: Someone who has been in a tech department. Uses a lot of technical details and jargon. Plays the purchasing role following step-by-step guides, wants to show his technical knowledge but needs the sales relationship to understand the market.

Those are the most common examples – you might also meet people with a combination of those approaches. The key message is, as they're different you also need to adjust your own style and approach to "fit" the puzzle. With that said, always be yourself and stick to your authenticity, don't pretend that you're someone else.

Adjust, adapt.

How do they "play" with their suppliers?

They make all kinds of analyses from the market, supplier landscape and they mix it with their market position and vision: some examples below:

Number of suppliers: They balance and play with outsiders to position for the next cycle. Testing supplier's strategy, relationship, and position/ranking. Shift volumes between first and second suppliers to keep them sharp. Are there new candidates? Who could be the substitutes for current suppliers?

They reevaluate volume divisions between partners, challengers, and outsiders.

Demand: They keep an eye out for growth. Optimization and reduction of volumes? Properly forecasted or too much market dependent? This too is relevant to get better terms.

They analyze their buying position. Are we a big, medium or small player? Very often they use Porter's Five Forces strategy:

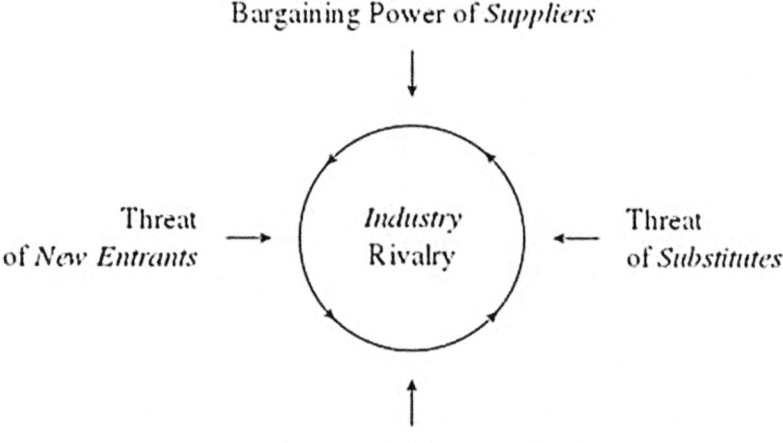

Source: Wikipedia By Denis Fadeev - Own work, CC BY-SA 3.0, https://commons.wikimedia.org/w/index.php?curid=32946157

The question you need to ask yourself and your organization is: do you know your position as a supplier? And take it from there, (is this the position we want to be in? Alternatives? Growth strategy? How can we...)

Your position as a supplier will depend on the type of products you're selling and what they represent to your customer as per the Kralijc Matrix:

Supply risk	Cost impact: Low	Cost impact: High
High	**Bottleneck Items** Need to ensure supply	**Strategic Items** Need to form partnerships
Low	**Non-Critical items** Make simple, automate	**Leverage items** minimize costs

Source: https://www.procurious.com/blog-content/2016/10/Kraljic-Categories.jpg

Pricing in the eyes of the purchaser:

Traditionally purchasers have two different price approaches, depending on their business and your products:

Value creation or cost plus

Undervalue creation: the purchasers are well aware that it leads to customization, where costs are not linked or related, therefore somehow more difficult to challenge the sellers that will follow "market conditions".

As for cost development, this will demand openness in the terms of levels of costs from both sides (often sellers are reticent about this, to link their offers with cost developments). Cost is the basis of negotiations (but not the only parameter). There are advantages for both, purchasers know the price evolution won't be arbitrary and market dependent, while the seller knows his margins will be stable and not suffer from negative market conditions.

Will purchasers clearly define their position? Not necessarily. If they do, great, you know where to start. If they don't, you can ask or simply test the waters by using different offers based on the two approaches, and checking with the customer what best fits his business. I have both types of customers and there's absolutely no problem to do it that way. Actually, I think a mix is a good balance of risk/rewards in terms of margin developments.

If the customer isn't aware of your costs, neither is he interested in cost elements, he's looking for an offer that matches their targets. If the customer is well aware of your costs and they do have an immediate effect on your offer, they need to be constantly mentioned but not as a sole element for price fixing. Very often customers following "cost plus" developments try to push sellers solely to cost developments. Always remind them that there are several parameters and market circumstances reflected in the pricing – there's not one single cost parameter.

Regular purchasing techniques to put pressure on sellers:

- Refusing, or rejecting the facts as something that sellers are making up.
- Delay the decision or postpone meetings.
- Try to put the final decision on management or under "analysis".
- Request more details and cost breakdown.
- Say they want to discuss the increase with your boss.
- Play it with your emotions.
- Say they can't pass the increase on to their customers.
- Need time to pass the increase through to their customers.

- Blaming you by saying that you should have warned them in advance and not come up with an increase at short notice.
- Play it as if they don't accept your increase at all.
- Try to bridge the burden and say you need to share part of the burden
- Warn that you are the only supplier coming up with this increase, you might put your supplying position at risk.
- Being accepting in their general attitude by understanding your point of view and position, but claiming that for sure you understand theirs as well. Proposing to meet halfway.

Main message wrap-up:

- Has targets and KPI's as you do, his role is to secure supply at the most suitable conditions.
- Different types of buyers: emotional, accountant, bossy, technical.
- Suppliers "homework": Number of suppliers, volume division, force competition among suppliers, Porter Five Competitive Forces, Kralijc matrix.
- Pricing on buyer view: value creation or cost plus
- Typical buying objections: not the right time, or price is too high. Need to discuss with production, we have enough suppliers, need more background of your offer in terms of costs.

PART II

The Deal Making Process

In this section, I'll take you through the different aspects, timing and steps of the deal-making process with its challenges and opportunities. Don't rush. Don't talk too much. Be a good listener and observer.

6

Preparation For A Meeting Or Negotiation

Here we are on the practical side of the sales manager's life. You've heard about the psychology of the role, the fact that you're unique, therefore no one can copy you. Can you copy other successful sales managers? Don't try to copy – it won't work. But learn, observe and adopt the way they work by being yourself. But now, reality knocks on the door and it's time to put all that into practice. How do you do your homework and prepare to face a challenging purchaser or a difficult negotiation? Nothing is difficult, but thinking it so, makes it so. Rarely, very rarely are there situations in B2B where there will be just one meeting, one shot, to make a deal. I'll underline it, it's about relationships, it's all about the long run. Of course, there will be some opportunities for a single deal, a one-time offer, but those will come and go. There are customers with weekly or monthly recurrent needs that will give you only one shot. Don't worry if you miss the first or some. That's part of the role.

Always remember, everything should be simple, but not simpler than it should. Anyone can make things complex. The key here or in any other area of life and business is, to make it simple. Very often salespeople tend to bring unnecessary complexity to the table or discussion. Normally that's just to hide their insecurity, hide the fact that they don't have a clear idea of the customer or their real needs. If you're not able to explain something in plain and simple words, you haven't mastered the subject. Another reason salespeople tend to add complexity to negotiations is (in their minds) to show they're knowledgeable and experts by using such complexity. Complex formulas or proposals sound pompous and superior. But the reality is, they don't – and they don't add any value. Purchasers will see them as unnecessary, as "fluff" or as hiding ruses. You don't need complexity to close a deal with the best results. Actually, the less complex the higher chance of positive results, as you will engage in less time, resources and ultimately costs, and the customer will be less overwhelmed with your offer.

So how do you prepare?

You need to tackle preparation from an internal and external perspective, meaning your side/company and purchaser/company.

If it's a first time meeting probably you don't have yet a good or enough information about the customer. No rush, you won't close a deal in your first meeting. If you do, something doesn't smell right. Preparation is key in sales. Using the old quote, failing to prepare is preparing for failure. At the same time, don't stay stick to a plan. The plan is important, but a flexible one, that can be adapted as long as the discussion goes.

Things you must be aware or practice beforehand:

- Body language, be always watchful of yours and your counterpart:
    - Occupy the scene (arms on the desk "grabbing terrain")
    - Crossed arms – indicates a defensive or closed mode.

- Eyes – maintain eye contact. Eye avoidance indicates evasion, building up stories
  - Facial expression: it should match your words.
  - Cordial or friendly expression, besides conveying empathy, leads the other person to follow.
- Tone, tenor, and pace of your voice:
  - Speak in a lower tone, but not too low.
  - Don't speak too quickly, you don't need to rush. Go slow, explain, detail.
  - Be a storyteller. Don't go from start to finish in the same tone, that gets boring. Emphasise some words, give them life.
- Your personal style
  - What kind of seller are you:
    - Hunter or farmer?
    - Adjust your style according to the kind of customer/prospect you have in front of you. But don't rush and don't aim to clearly position yourself as either a hunter or a farmer.
    - Learn to listen. Shut up and listen. Don't talk just to fill the emptiness. Silence is very often more valuable than words.

Things you should know in advance (or find out as soon as possible, before stepping into the negotiation phases):

- Your customer classification:
  - What represents the customer for you?
    - Key account? Key development account? Maintenance account? Opportunistic?

- - Based on what you know or what you think you know?
  - Is there potential to explore further? Have there been changes in their business?
- What kind of supplier/position is yours at the customer?
  - Support/Aggressor (low volumes)
  - Challenger (reasonable volumes)
  - Partner (big volumes)
  - Do you want to keep that position? What would you need to do to change it?
- What type of product is yours (in your customer's eyes):
  - Routine items? they have a low financial impact and low supply risk so customers won't spend a lot of time on them.
  - Leverage Items: they have a higher financial impact but low supply risk. There will be bargaining.
  - Bottle-neck items: they have a low financial impact but high supply risk so there will be some caution on the side of the customer. They need to be assured of supply. Explore that specific aspect.
  - Strategic items: these have both a financial impact and relevant supply risk, so that's where the customer will spend most of his time and engage in relationships.
- Awareness of the negotiation steps
  - Preparation/Discussion/Proposals/Bargaining/Agreement
    - Not necessarily in this order – not necessarily in order at all – buyer can drag you back and forth – but at least be aware of this and what is involved in each step. Don't bargain before

having made your proposal, don't show your proposal while you're still discussing. Rushing can make you lose potential negotiation margins and weaken your position.

- Type of buyer (emotional, accountant, bossy, technical)
- Customer category (sole local buyer, purchasing department with different elements, global purchasing organization, group purchasing)
- Decision-making tree (technical staff, production staff, marketing staff, finance department)
- Competition landscape of customer market (main customer competitors, trends, market share per player, product life cycles)
- Customer alternatives (suppliers, alternative materials, imports, product optimization)
- Buyer purchasing cycle/periods/routine (irregular? Market driven? Seasonal? Monthly? Campaigns? Annually?)

The opposite aims of Buyers and Sellers:

Buyers	Sellers
Simple relationship	Strategic relationship
Low costs	Higher costs
Multiple suppliers	Sole supplier
Lowest Market price	Market price is a vague concept
Cost + thinking	Value
Specialities to commodity	Sell commodities as specialties

- The meeting premise – before you hit the road have this very

clear:
- Purpose (why this meeting?)
- Objective (result expected)
- Premise (what do we know about the customer?)
- Strategy (How will we achieve expected result?)
- Anticipate (what might the customer require?)

Main message wrap-up:

- Body language, voice (tone, tenor, pace)
- Adapt your personal style to your counterpart
- Customer classification
- What kind of supplier are you in customer's eyes/needs?
- What does your product represent to the customer?
- The negotiation steps
- What kind of purchasing organization? Who's the decision maker/influencer? What type of buyer?
- Customer alternatives
- Customer buying cycles

7

The Meeting: How To Lead It

There are a few key aspects you need to be aware of and be very attentive to. These will help you to have a clear view of what's happening and control the discussion or its course (or at least not let yourself fall in the customer trap. Remember, until you gain his trust and are able to build up a cordial relationship with your customer/buyer, he will challenge you, shake you, almost ignore you and for sure test all boundaries. On the one hand, you need to be in control of yourself but also control the direction of the discussion.

Often, you have your agenda and you're expecting the discussion to follow a certain order and direction, and consequently attain a certain outcome. But then, once you start, the customer will bring up all kinds of diversions and will lead you in all kinds of directions – bringing to the table topics that you weren't expecting and mixing up all the steps of the agenda. There are two possible reasons for this. First, the purchaser is hectic and disorganized and can't follow good order and preparation – there are a few – sometimes who do this just to show you how busy they are and how complicated their lives are. The second one is a bit trickier. Purchasers will do that on purpose. To confuse you, to drain your energy, to put you off the rails and forget your main objective. It's part of their strategy. Don't let yourself fall into that trap.

To avoid that, you must keep the following in mind:

- Send a clear agenda in advance.
    - All points to be discussed, in a sequential order

- Inform who's going from your side, ask who will attend on their end.
- Ask them if they have any other points to add to the agenda
- Ask them if they need any info or material in advance (sales specifications, GTC's, technical data sheets, etc.)
- The expected duration of the meeting

- What kind of buyer are you facing?
- How is the "power balance"?
  - He knows things you don't know, but you also know things he doesn't know. Information is power, and every side will try to use it in its favor.
  - The good thing is, he doesn't know what you know and what you don't know.
  - Customers don't know everything.

Don't let yourself be overwhelmed if he uses a power play with his customer position or market information. He needs you as much as you need him – and you know many things he doesn't. Power play is just a bluff.

- Put your emotions aside:
  - It's about positions, not people. Even if the customer uses and abuses the pronoun "you", it's not about you. It's just a means to put you under pressure.
- Active listening: listen, not with the intention to answer right away, but to understand.
  - Very often salespeople think that if they don't answer immediately they're perceived as not being knowledgeable and will lose their image. Wrong. You don't need to comment or answer on the spot. That normally happens when you're not focused and let your ego and emotions get in the way. Let your silence

kill their enthusiasm. Silence will put doubts in their heads.

- Don't rush and jump immediately on any proposal or what you think about the deal. Hold your horses.
- It's about what they want/need in the first place.
    - They don't care what you want. It's your work to bridge their wants with your solutions and close eventual gaps. That's the negotiation process. Very often salespeople get so focused on their expectations that they forget the bigger picture and the purpose of a discussion. It's a dialogue, not a monologue.
- Are there any gatekeepers (people who are not supportive like technical or production? If yes, also involve your own counterparts with their expertise to dissipate their resistance). Let technical people speak with technical people. They have a special language of their own.

During the discussion, it's important that you ask the right questions and clear all areas of doubt about how to optimize this deal/customer.

In that sense, there's an important thing to be aware of: there are no stupid questions, eventually, there are only stupid answers. Ask. Don't be afraid to ask, even at a later stage when you have been dealing with the customer for a while. **Assumption is one of the biggest mistakes we can make in sales.** Assuming that the customer needs this or that service (as that's the industry standard), assuming the customer won't accept short payment terms, assuming the customer has many alternatives. Stop it. Don't assume anything at all. Ask. Every customer is different. You might find many similarities, but one deviation might have a relevant impact on the way you do business with A or X, or on what's really relevant for each customer.

So keep the meeting going this way:

- Let the customer speak. Don't interrupt him. The more he talks, the better. As a rule of thumb, the customer should speak 70% of the time and the seller 30%. When a customer is so eager to speak, he can share information, from the market, from his company, from the competition. That's an excellent source. Feed his ego and you'll have a lot of material to broaden your view of his business and position.

- Ask open questions. This is particularly useful when you have a purchaser that isn't a big mouth. It's rare but can happen. In general, purchasers like to show they know better than you and talk a lot. If they don't, ask them as many open questions as possible.

- Bring the discussion to the topics you want: very often a purchaser will send fireworks in all directions. Every now and then, bring them back to the discussion. Keep the focus on the aim of your meeting.

- What are their top requirements from a supplier in order of relevance? On-time delivery, packaging solution, quick response, price, payment terms, consignment stock, you name it. Very often salespeople assume the customer's first and second priority is price and payment terms. Let me tell you one thing. That's what you assume, and eventually, that's what customers will tell you. Nevertheless, in my extensive sales experience, the customer's main concern – when we're talking about strategic or bottleneck items – is not price or payment terms, but having the product or services on time to run their company. This is the purchaser's main concern. Of course, he needs to watch his budget and will put pressure on prices, but imagine what happens if he fails to have the product in-house? A production halt because he didn't ensure delivery of enough raw materials on time? All his company calling and wondering why the product isn't there?

- Ask or confirm in detail what the deal is about and all its premises to avoid any misunderstanding or grey zones. Often times purchasers leave some grey zones on purpose when presenting a deal so that later on they can explore it in their favor. Or after you have made a proposal, they come up with additional requirements. This is a typical behavior, so avoid it as much as possible and be very clear about what your offer is covering.

- Again, no rush. You don't have to provide an offer on the spot. Bring home as many details as possible and tell the customer you'll study a proposal that you'll send in a few days. Tell them you need to work carefully on the proposal so it's competitive enough.

- Don't forget an important aspect: keep your promises. Don't overpromise. Over deliver. So if you promise an offer in five days, send it in three. Keeping your word is key to building trust and long-term relationships. If, for whatever reason, you foresee along the way that it won't be possible (for instance you need to wait for manager's green light and he's not around) inform the customer in advance. Not on the last day.

- Visit report: After the meeting/visit, share a short summary of the discussion with the customer. This can be taken out of your internal visit report, and it's important to keep it short, clean and lean. Cut the crap. Only what matters to the customer and your ongoing negotiations or agreements:

    o -What you have agreed

    o -Topics that were closed

    o -What are the pending actions and on whom (yourself or him)?

    o -Any next steps or follow-ups.

The purchaser's role isn't to make your life easier. His role is to push you, to confuse you, to object to your arguments, to throw info you are unaware of, and to bring onto the table eventual weaknesses of your company (known from public, market or from previous experiences).

He does this to tire you so you lower your guard and start thinking he might be right and he's entitled to a better price, service or package. That's his role, at least until you get confidence enough or develop a trustworthy relationship where only what matters will be discussed – and without diversion games.

Main message wrap-up:

- Share a clear agenda with the customer beforehand.
- Put emotions aside. It's not personal.
- Listen. If not clear, ask again. Listen to what he says but also what he doesn't say, or what is between the lines.
- Encourage the buyer to talk.
- Don't assume anything. Ask, verify, confirm.
- Don't let the buyer mess up your agenda, keep in control, bring him to the main discussion.
- Don't overpromise, over deliver instead.
- No rush. You don't have to make the offer just now. Digest all the info and come back to him later. No customer is desperate to close the deal in one meeting. If he does or wants that, it's not a good sign or is just a means to pressure you.
- Share the meeting main points and outcome. Short and sweet. Closed topics, open actions, follow-ups.

8

The Offer

| Preparation | Discussion | Proposals | Bargaining | Deals |

Here you have to do your core work. Gather all the pieces you've been collecting so far to build up your proposal in such a way that it can be competitive enough and bring the best returns to your company. Have in mind the items below to prepare your offer:

- How important is the customer?
    - What's your best alternative to this customer in terms of volume, returns, logistics, resources and so on?
    - What is your strategic intent?
        - This is just an account to be used on/off.
        - This is a "farming" account – good margins/low level of demand.
        - This is a key development account.
        - This is a potential strategic partner/key account.
    - Is there something specific that makes him special and justify lower margins? For instance, a trendsetter or a very technological customer that can be of high interest for your own technical and marketing people

- Pricing

    - Don't rush with price offers. Customers will ask you right from the beginning "What's your price?" Hold off and explain to them you don't have a price but value to discuss, and that will depend on several factors and their specific needs, it's not a supermarket approach. You will provide them with a proposal, according to their different needs, and requests vs costs involved (volume, packaging, payment terms, product rotation, logistics, technical support, regulatory documents etc.)

    - Make sure you're not leaving money on the table. Don't give more than you need (in price or in service)

    - Don't offer too low or don't use huge price reductions to capture business or to steal customers from the competition. You'll just set a precedent and start what can turn into a price spiral (with your competition) and a bad habit. Customers will wonder, "If you did it once, you can do it more often." Your product/services should never be based on low prices. Find other differentiators; other features or other reasons to not let yourself roll into that trap. Price should never be the reason to acquire or lose business (within certain boundaries, of course).

    - Yes, you can use rebate schemes and loyalty rewards, but always in exchange for something – in most cases to reward volume commitment.

    - Transparency: be careful with customers that ask you the cost breakdown. This seems like a very well-intentioned question to know your costs, but it will turn against you sooner or later. Customer will start asking you about cost A, then cost B and so on; so it will be used not to understand your constraints, but to challenge you later on. If it's really difficult to push the customer away for whatever reason, the best you can do is provide "buckets" of costs, not individually. This way you'll always have a margin for maneuver later on. For instance "handling, logistics, and bagging". If they want to cancel or reduce one service, they don't know its exact cost and can't ask you that level of reduction on the price. You remain in charge.

- Price challenge: one good way to prevent price challenges (besides any concession you might have already in mind) is to come up with two price proposals, based on two different backgrounds. Again here you need to be clever to not simply cut one feature of the main offer and make the second one 10% lower. They will find out the cost of that item and challenge you in the future. As said before, have more than one feature differing from both offers. For instance, one is the "standard" offer with all the usual quality and service, while the second offer is based on ex-works and shorter payment terms (just as an example). Be pragmatic and keep it simple. Customers will try to push you for a third option (Option A plus one item from offer B). Just cut it out and tell them it's not possible. Whenever you use this approach, be sure that any challenge can be immediately put aside in a reasonable manner, or used in your favor.

- Value selling / Value proposition:
  - Don't use the statement, "I'll make you an offer based on value proposition" too early. Not until you know and understand what value means for them. You might think or assume a certain premise is in their interest, and it might turn that you're completely wrong. Remember what I said earlier about assumptions? You risk hearing, "You don't know my needs or problems, how can you make me a value proposition?" Do this only when you have enough

customer info and background to approach the customer from that angle.

- Don't provide prices, use the word "value" instead of price. I can buy something for $50 but its value (for me) can be much higher than that, therefore I'll feel I made a great deal. I sold a motorbike for a price of $2K, but its value (for me) was much higher. The key is to find what does the customer values and how high they rate it

- Make your proposal based on the customer's real needs, not based on your assumptions and what the market generally uses. This is a very common mistake nowadays; companies over deliver services or qualities that the customer doesn't require. Fine-tuning on both sides, with no need to price higher but reducing costs, would bring the same margins while keeping prices competitive.

- Make a value proposition when you clearly know the pain or hurdle of a customer:

    - Small storage capacity and you're able to rotate the deliveries twice as fast to avoid a stock-out. This has a cost but the customer might be willing to pay, thinking about the benefits it brings.

    - Replace two or three different products with one that can fit all requirements. This will take away handling, time and resources on the customer's side, therefore can be used as a value proposition – fit for purpose offer.

- Commodities vs Specialties:

    - There are slight differences when you're selling a commodity or a specialty. Specialties are normally tailor-made or more complex to track back costs (and therefore final price) from the customer's perspective. Commodities are goods or services readily available in the market, where your product doesn't differ from any other supplier, therefore it's quite easy to benchmark the market price as often there are market indexes. Specialties are a different story. Example of a specialty is a flavor enzyme whereas naphtha or propylene are commodities. Salespeople on the commodity side are using different wording, such as "standard products" to avoid a negative or simplistic regard from the purchaser. But let's be honest, they're not naïve. On the service side, you'll find similar approaches with "standard services" or "premium services".

- o There are several pricing structures or solutions:
    - Spot/recurrent negotiated prices (opportunistic sales)
    - Fixed price for a certain period/quantity (price in exchange of upfront agreed volumes, time or usage)
    - Formula prices based on market index plus (normally for long-term agreements)
    - Formula prices based on few key indexes with variation limitations (long-term agreements)
    - Formula price based on cost index plus (long-term agreements)

- The Negotiation steps
    - o Bear in mind that in almost any negotiation, there are certain steps you will go through. Do you have to go through all of them? Not necessarily. Depending on the negotiation and your relationship with the customer some steps can be avoided (on purpose or simply not needed). Do you have to go through it in

sequential mode as presented below? No. Also here, there can be a shift between one step or another. What's important is that the final step *is* the final step. Once you get there, don't go back and forth. If you do that, it means bargaining or proposals weren't properly done and closed. Remember, buyers are experts and are pushing you out of your order to disturb you. They will push you from the beginning, "But what's your price?" Don't go into pricing or offers until you feel you have covered all parameters and info needed to do so. You can never tell a price when you don't know all the premises, all the requirements, all the conditions (and I underline it once more), very often only after knowing your price customers will tell you, "Ah but I also want this and that." or "I thought that was including X feature."

- Preparation
  - Business, people, interests, options, criteria
- Discussion
  - Develop trust, don't assume, ask, listen, encourage them to ask, be clear, no proposals yet
- Proposals
  - If...then. Fill it as much as possible on the best and worst case scenario, before you come up with your proposal
- Bargaining
  - Keep your concessions, rank them in terms of value in the customer's eyes, start with the one he perceives as the most valuable. One at a time, no rush.

- Agreement
  - Have it clear, and have it closed. Don't allow grey zones or the chance to get cold feet. Clearly show what your offer covers.

Don't forget this key item:

As stated in the Buyer chapter, it's in the purchaser's DNA to object, delay, make you feel uncomfortable and power play during the negotiation.

If they object – and they will – it's extremely important that you ask as many details as possible to any objection, so you can cover it with a solution or a concession but don't allow the customer to divert and come back with another objection later on. Asking them very clearly what, how, who, when, why Keeps them away to close the deal today.

- It didn't go that well? You feel lost and need help?
  - You're a bit overwhelmed, as the customer made some unconventional requirements and you don't know how to handle them? Take it easy:
    - This is not a lonely ride. Very often salespeople take it too personally and feel it's their responsibility to solve all problems. This is a noble attitude, but you're not alone nor are you supposed to master things you are not aware of. Call for help. It's not a sign of weakness, it's a sign of responsibility and courage.
    - Your success is the success (or failure) of your sales director. He's more than interested that you succeed and overcome any hurdle. Involve him whenever something passes your limitations. But also ask for advice.

- Technical and marketing people are also there for you, eager to add value and overcome challenges. Use them.
- Sales colleagues: most likely they have already faced the same kind of issues. Check with them about their experience.

The sales manager role is quite independent. Folks are responsible to manage their portfolios on their own and as their own business – following mandates and business guidelines – bringing the desired results home, but any complex customer or difficult negotiation will benefit from team support. Exchange. Share best practices. That's also part of the sales manager's role, the capacity to help and support colleagues to achieve the company's targets.

Main message wrap-up:

- Yours and the customer's strategic intent
- What kind of buyer/purchasing are your dealing with?
- What's your best alternative?
- Follow the negotiation steps
- Don't rush offering a price too early
- What pricing structure to use?
- Keep the concessions in your pocket, have them ranked per customer perception. Start with the more important ones. Use only one at the time and try to stick there.
- Ask for help if you feel lost or confused, it's not a sign of weakness but of responsibility and courage. Would it be better to lose the deal?

9

The Follow Up

The offer is done and you're waiting impatiently for the feedback. Time for suspense and a bit of anxiety. By now, there's no more bargain or negotiation. There are two scenarios:

- You won the deal. Great. You're happy and a bit relieved. Then you think you probably could have asked for more...but don't look back from that angle. That one is done, start thinking about the next occasion. But still...

- **If the deal is in your pocket:**
    - Honor it. Don't just celebrate and turn your back. A deal is a deal, so whatever the future brings, don't come back in the middle saying, "You know the conditions changed a lot in the meantime and we need to revise our offer." Unless in real Force major cases and still, this will have a very negative impact on your reputation.
    - It's also very important that you ensure the deal is executed according to the agreements (by both sides). So follow up on how the deal is being delivered, and how things are going. Don't just leave it to the operational people. The customer doesn't know your operational people or anyone else. You are the company's face. If anything goes sideways, it's your reputation, reliability, and trustworthiness that is at stake for the next negotiation.

- Even if everything is going according to the terms of the agreement, and let's say, the deal is for a long period such as one year, don't disconnect with the customer during this time. Keep the contact, keep exchanging information, keep showing interest in the customer, keep "defending your position." Don't forget that the competition is at the door doing the same thing.

- Reinforce the application of the clauses and premises of the deal. Very often, after the start of the implementation and deliveries, customers will play with volume placement, and if it's to their advantage (better conditions from elsewhere) will order much less than agreed. Follow that up, and push the customer to follow the agreement or you'll have to cancel or revise it. Often customers throw out a big volume during negotiations just to benefit from a good price and conditions, but later, depending on how best it suits them comparing to market developments, they place volumes/orders below minimum levels.

- In case the agreement isn't being respected by the customer regularly (one-off can happen as long as properly pre-discussed), you need to warn them about the contract cancelations and/or penalties. Don't just let customers use the contract as a lever for their side without proper returns or compensations to your end.

- **If the customer replied with the well-known sentence, "We regret to inform you," then the deal is lost. Don't turn your back, don't drop it, don't feel you failed. You didn't. They simply had a better offer or weren't sure about yours. So this is not the end, but the beginning:**

  - For sure it's not pleasant, but take the best out of each situation. Is there any positive sign of losing a deal? Yes, probably not immediately, but when the results of feedback are properly dissected they can provide you with relevant information that can't be ignored and will help you for future negotiations. Start preparing for their next buying cycle.

- Don't just assume you lost the deal because your price is too high. Start looking around at everything else. If the end price was the sum of a few things, what are those things? Where could you possibly improve?

- Ask for as much feedback as possible about why you're not the chosen one. Often it's not about the price, but payment terms, proximity, or features you can't offer (for instance, consignment stock), reliability, technical support, fewer hurdles with operational matters. This info is crucial for you to prepare for the next opportunity.

- Don't just drop the customer and wait for the next round/year. Once in a while, get in touch, check how things are going, check if there is additional demand. Check if there have been any changes in people or organization. Show that your interest isn't solely on closing one deal but on keeping a relationship and proximity with the customer.

- Keep your foot in the door, you never know if (for whatever reason) they're not happy with their chosen supplier – and you could be just the right guy to step in.

- By keeping in touch and gathering info, you're preparing yourself to tackle any gaps that you had previously.

Main message wrap-up:

- **Deal is in your pocket:**
    - A deal is a deal. Honour your deals, don't change terms along the way
    - The deal isn't the end of anything but the beginning. Follow up the implementation of the deal and keep in contact with the customer by exchanging market info. Secure your position for the next time.
    - Reinforce the application of the terms, don't let the customer play with volumes or repeatedly stay short on their promises.
- Deal is lost. Great, let's learn and gather as much info as possible for the next time/round:
    - Don't assume anything at all. You'll be prone to assume it was due to price. Don't assume, ask for feedback, as much and as detailed as possible.
    - Even if the price is the visible part of the iceberg, don't stay there. What's beneath? What costs could you improve? What services are you offering that the customer didn't ask for or need? What features are you missing? How can you improve product performance?
    - Don't just drop your arms and wait for next year/round. Keep showing up, keep the contact. You never know if the winning supplier is messing up and you could take his position.
    - You'll have one year, month or whatever the period is, to fix your minus points and place yourself well positioned for the next period. If you just lose contact and try back later, you won't have the chance to improve and close that gap.

PART III

The Practicality

In this section, I'll provide you with a set of tools, guides and support material. This is where theory meets practice. It's the rest of your toolbox to get you properly equipped to face any purchaser.

10

Most Relevant Tools, Systems Or Tasks

In this section, I'll enumerate some of the most common tools and systems that are part of the sales executive role; some of them on a daily basis, some of them periodic. Some of them directly related to your fieldwork, others more related to the reporting and corporate memory, but all relevant to allow your maximum contribution to the company strategy and results.

With the increasing relevance and use of technology, some of them might be more in use or trending than others. Be aware that, for some specific markets or industry segments there are a couple of new "hi-tech" things popping up. I like technology and try as much as possible to keep an eye on any relevant development, though, as usual, there's a lot of noise around new things that in reality, just don't fit in most of the businesses, aren't used or are used inappropriately, which leads to unnecessary hurdles. Let's take Twitter, for instance, it might not be a relevant tool for big B2B corporations in the gas/oil/chemical world, but can be extremely important for SaaS companies. So, there's no right or wrong, and don't take the below information as unique, but as the most commonly-used platforms in the various fields:

- EMAIL/OUTLOOK:
    - Sounds logical and at the same time one of the most critical aspects of life for a salesperson. A big part of his time and activity will be spent with this tool. Therefore, I'd strongly recommend you to organize it

properly at the onset. The time you might spend organizing folders, archives and favorites will be a benefit to you with quick access, quick archive, quick retrieval of info or old emails. The number of folders won't stop growing (hopefully with the growth of customer portfolios and prospects) so the better you have things organized, the more productive you'll become. Each person has his own way to work. Find yours, but don't just let yourself go with the flow, it will cost you time, efficiency and energy at a later stage.

- o Create folders for each customer, internal stakeholders or departments.

- o Create rules to auto-archive or organize incoming and outgoing emails.

- o Use flags and reminders to prioritize your pending actions.

- o Use calendar for follow up emails/actions.

- SENSING QUESTIONNAIRE (OR APPROACH) – Template available on my webpage:

    - o It might differ from company to company, but the basis of sales management relies on understanding customers and adapting products and services to their needs. However, identifying these needs constitutes a highly challenging task. Very often we assume and make conclusions based on what's said or visible on the surface, or we just keep the business running without asking ourselves basic questions. A sensing questionnaire/exercise can hugely improve your knowledge about the customer and can help you adapt your proposals and offers to their specific needs and not just make offers based on assumptions.

- FORECASTING:
    - Forecasting is crucial, particularly in the industry as it allows for proper planning and optimization of utilization rates, but also in any other business with stock optimization and product rotation. By gathering direct info from your customers, based on historical and recurrent volumes or expectations according to market dynamics (seasonal impacted businesses, for instance) that input is required in most corporations on a periodical basis (monthly or quarterly). Don't confuse this with budget or sales plans. One thing is that your targets or expectations set at the begging of the year or period, another is the reality of a given moment.

- VISIT REPORTS: Template available on my webpage
    - Every company will have its own process or way of working. In some, there's a standard format or template, while in others, there's no obligation or strict rule about visit reports. One way or the other, for your own sake and organization – also if one day you need to hand over the customer or the entire portfolio to another colleague – I'd strongly recommend that you record and store your important meetings or visits, even if you don't share them with anyone. In many cases, the visit reports are sent to the Sales Director. Some companies use CRM integrated systems, while others are adverse to such technology. No right or wrong, as long as it serves the purpose of the business and is not just a "tick the box" exercise.
    - One unnecessary mistake I see often in visit reports is the inclusion of too much company details and data. There are tools and systems to capture that info. Keep the visit report sharp and to the point. A visit report is

not an Account Plan (but might be an action of the AP).

- LEAD GENERATION: Template available on my webpage

    o Again, each company will have its own system or database. If it doesn't, there are currently free platforms online or you can create a rough spreadsheet or your own database. Every business must have a customer pipeline as no customer is for granted. Every year, customers come and go. Be ready for that. Always fill the customer pipeline and search potential new customers and be ready to replace a departing customer, to replace an under-performing customer, or to grow your sales. Keep this updated. The lead generation is an ongoing exercise, not something you do once a year. Here you can use the customer checklist and assessment to qualify your leads. There are several names or labels for this exercise, so if you come across things like "Customer pipeline", "Prospecting", "Growth platform" we're talking basically about the same thing.

- SALES VISIT PREPARATION: Template available on my webpage

    o This framework helps you to prepare for a customer visit. The purpose, the objective, the premise, the strategy and the anticipation. This exercise is crucial for non-routine visits. You need to know, prepare, gather facts and anticipate. Ahead of any meeting, check all these points. It's not a waste of time. Don't just have in mind what you want or need. It's not about what you want, but the starting point is what the customer wants. Don't just think, "Along the way, I'll prepare for the visit". Nope, along the way you can't check data, review open action points, or remember some of the customer specifics.

- BATNA: Template available on my webpage
    - Are you selling to the best customers? At the best price? Or are there other alternatives that could bring the same or better returns with fewer costs? How do you know that? This tool or process allows you to benchmark not only internally with your existing portfolio and the possible alternatives to a customer, but also your position as their supplierand their alternative among the different competitors. Doing that exercise as carefully as possible (using facts and figures) will allow you to define your position and eventually determine the margin you can aim for or the magnitude of concessions you can make.

- Contact Matrix: Template available on my webpage
    - Do you know "who is who" in the company? The technical manager, the project manager, the quality manager? Finance? How can you put them in direct contact with their counterpart in your company? Gather this info, it can be very useful and unlock negotiations. Don't limit your contacts only to the purchaser. Often he's a sort of gatekeeper, or he pretends he has the power when other departments or functions are the real decision makers. The contact matrix is often supported or followed up by the Decision/Influence Matrix. But not always.

- Influence Matrix:
    - Do you know who your customer's decision-makers really are? Who influences who? Who blocks who? Who supports what?
    - With this "box" you can capture the different stakeholders, their diverse level of influence on decisions, and match them internally with your respective peers. For instance, their technical manager. What's the relevance of his input? Can he

influence the buyer?

- o Once the decision-making unit is known, it's also important to define – if needed – individual goals, roles, obligations and work plans. Take this example: your technical colleague manages to influence your customer's technical department regarding the benefits of your product. What will happen next? They will influence the purchaser in your favor.

- The Adopters Curve:

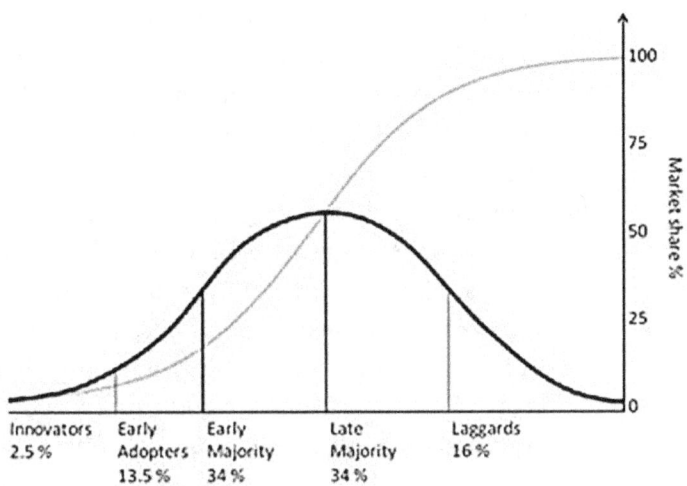

Source By Rogers Everett - Based on Rogers, E. (1962) Diffusion of innovations. Free Press, London, NY, USA., Public Domain, https://commons.wikimedia.org/w/index.php?curid=18525407

- o Product lifecycle. A new product will go through a different sequence of stages from its introduction towards its decline. This curve is normally used by marketing teams but it's always good to know its existence and principles as you'll experience this evolution on your customer's portfolio.

- SELLING Models:
  - I need to touch base on this one, as particularly with technology boost, we might tend to think that B2B sales need a specific label – otherwise it seems obsolete. We hear so many different selling models that we tend to feel uncomfortable as we don't even know what they are about or if we're working with nineteen-century tools. As explained earlier, in my view and experience, sales don't happen by following a script. With that said, every sales organization should have their own process or system. Is this confusing? No. I'm saying that selling is not about knowing a process, but having the right person knowing a process and executing it. The danger of having a process is the risk of thinking that you can grab anyone intelligent, get him to read the process, and you'll have a great sales executive. Conclusion: people are far more important than the process. Just for reference, here are some of the most common or well-known selling models. Did I ever use them? No. Or probably I did use pieces and bits of one and the other, not even being aware of it.
  - You might hear or come across one of these:
    - Conceptual selling
    - Consultative selling
    - SPIN selling
    - Solution selling
    - Dale Carnegie Sales
    - Sales First
    - And hundreds more....

    My opinion is that if they were so efficient you'd have only a few, but as it happens, as in many other areas, there is no one-fits-all model, and you risk getting lost with the offer, not knowing which one to follow and whether you should follow any at all. They all have pros and cons.

But don't panic with such a wide range of offers, you can easily segregate them into two groups:

- Based on presentations
    - This is the old school model. Sharing information about the products a company has to offer. Talk, talk, talk.
- Based on questions:
    - This is the new school. As it gets much easier to access info with the internet and technology, customers already know what's out there. This approach is based on raising the right questions. Ask, ask, ask. Here the customer talks, the seller listens and deals with information received

Even if a company doesn't have a defined or "labeled" sales model, most likely they're using one of the above approaches (or even a combination of both).

One last thing, you don't have to worry if you don't know exactly what the selling model of your company is. Those labels count for little in the real world. Do you think the customer will ask you or care which selling model you're using?

I've worked for major corporations in the oil, gas and chemical industry. Some do have their own selling model, others don't use any specific or use parts of one or the other, just a sales strategy following the marketing plan and sales plan.

CRM systems:

- This is a data warehouse system to capture customer's key information, insights, and interactions. Normally accessible by sales, marketing, and management.
- When used properly, this tool is very helpful and powerful to increase customer satisfaction, retention, and fuel growth.
- If it is so important, why is there so much resistance on the part of sales executives to use it?
  - There is poor communication and information across the different functions and from top management on the benefits and the proper handling of the tool.
  - Salespeople are asked to be productive, close deals quickly, and avoid distractions. Therefore they see CRM as a waste of time and resources.
  - The CRM is an IN/OUT system. The quality of the information is based on the quality of the reports.
  - Any major info, development or interaction with Sales, Marketing or any other department should be captured here for future follow up, reference, action and even corporate memory.
  - This is not an "archive" system, but a tool that should be used and updated regularly.

- SOCIAL SELLING
  - This is a software that helps salespeople initiate and build relationships with buyers on social media sites such as Twitter, Linkedin, Facebook or Snapchat. Most people, though, use social media sites on a personal

level. Again, for some industries, this might be important, but for many others, the likelihood that you can start any engagement here is quite low as they are more reticent to technology or perceive these channels as not fitting their business model. But they're definitely a good source of information, engagement, and connection.

- EMAIL TRACKING:
    - It's a software that integrates with your email and allows you to know when a recipient opens an email or opens a link you've sent.

- GOOGLE ALERTS:
    - You can set up alerts to track what competitors are doing, your specific market news, topics, people, and even follow your prospects' activities.

- Cloud systems
    - Dropbox, Google Drive, and Amazon Cloud, among others. This is one piece of technology that any business and teams can't ignore. Mobility, file sharing, sharing folders, links and so on.

- EVERNOTE:
    - One of the salesperson's main problems is taking notes, organizing them, sharing them or archiving them. Evernote takes care of this and much more - like sharing or voice recording when you're out of paper or driving.

Main message wrap-up:

- Email/Outlook
- Sensing questionnaire
- Forecasting
- Visit report
- Lead generation
- Visit preparation
- BATNA
- Contact matrix
- Influence matrix
- Adopters curve
- Selling models
- CRM systems
- Social selling
- Email tracking
- Google alerts
- Cloud systems
- Evernote
- Rapportive

11

Sales Executive First Months PLAN

In principle, when you're assigned a sales role, there should be an onboard plan to provide you with the knowledge (processes, systems), training (product or service training), information (customer portfolio and leads), targets (volume, margin, DSO, Overdue, HSSE, etc), mandatory training (compliance, anti-trust) and other high level information such as company vision and strategy, competition landscape, sales strategy and positioning, growth plans and many other basics to get you equipped properly.

Well, that's the usual procedure, though it might also happen that due to whatever reason – there's no time, no process in place, no onboarding plan – you're just thrown into the arena. What happens then?

Two possible scenarios:

- The company asks you to come up with a kind of 90-day plan

    Or

- You do it spontaneously and share it with your management. This shows you're organized, take initiative and like to work based on an initial plan, even if it will need to be adjusted along the way.

My suggestion is, if the company doesn't provide you with any plan and no specific onboard training, you build a "First months plan" to help you focus and have clarity on the way to go. Focus on nothing specific and you'll be distracted by everything.

At the same time, be reasonable, don't shoot yourself in the foot. B2B sales demands time and patience, and in my opinion, it takes more than six months for you to be up and running (depending on your previous experience in sales, product, company knowledge and market specifics). But of course, a company can't wait six months to get you out there reaching your customers, so this initial period will be demanding and you won't feel very comfortable, but that's what we call "learning on the job", the most efficient learning process. Just for guidance, here are some of the priorities I would put in a 90-day plan:

- Find out what or how your market looks like:
    - Competition
    - Market share per player
    - Your company weaknesses and strengths
- Know your products/services
    - Ask the technical, marketing or production colleagues for some training.
- Get acquainted and start building relationships with your customers - **This is probably the absolute priority**
    - Historical data and relationships
    - Customer potential and your share
    - Customer perception of you, as a supplier
    - Customer expectations of you, as a supplier
- Ask to be introduced (or do it yourself) to your organization and key stakeholders. (Key in the sense of their relevance to support you in your day-to-day role, not as senior stakeholders who could leverage your career, at least not yet):
    - Customer support center
    - Logistics
    - Credit

- o Technical staff
- o Product management
    - Having a good relationship with those above from the very beginning is crucial.

By the end of the 90 days you should able to have your own "map" and define the strategy to take the best out of your region/portfolio, albeit aligned with your targets and sales plan:

- Accounts to explore growth
- Accounts to manage, milk or farm
- Accounts in the need of building trust
- Accounts to drop or spend less energy on
- Regions or areas underdeveloped
- Plans and targets in terms of business development/leads

But I have to be honest, 90 days is a rather short period to implement this plan. It depends on the size of your portfolio and a few additional parameters, such as if you're dealing with commodities or specialties, an existent and mature market/products, or something recent, expensive items/services or low priced items. So there's no right/wrong if you make this a 90- or 180-day plan, as long as you back it up with facts. Always deal with facts. If you start with no info at all and you have to make assumptions along the way, confirm or amend those assumptions and move the cursor in the right direction. A good plan is a flexible plan. It doesn't matter how or where you create your path, as long as it delivers the expected results.

Main message wrap-up:

- Get an overview of your market:
- Know your products/services
- Start building relationships with your customers
- Get acquainted with your organization and key stakeholders. (Key in the sense of their relevance to support you in your day-to-day role, not as senior stakeholders that could leverage your career).
- Create a flexible plan, where you will tackle initial assumptions and adjust your course along the way.

12

MOST COMMON Sales Clichés

Some purchasers are so used to hearing them that they will laugh in your face when you use them. But there will be times that you'll not understand why the purchaser is laughing when you're telling him a certain reality. Well, the problem is that sales clichés have been overused. They are often not true or not properly backed up with facts so that now they sound to purchasers like a scratched vinyl disk or an old cassette playing the same song. So whenever you think of any of them, to avoid being laughed at, use facts and market info and try to avoid clichés.

I don't discourage you to use them, but when you do, please find the right context and sustain your sentence with concrete and substantial facts or info, otherwise, you'll fall short on arguments and it won't help you to close the deal. Here are some of the most commonly used sales rep clichés:

- **Market is short.** There's a strong demand and some producers are currently in the maintenance of their units. So this unbalanced offer/demand situation leads to a price increase.
    - Use it when it's really the case, not when you are short as a producer and the overall market has plenty of material. Provide info on which players are out, or which season or effect is supporting the strong demand

- This is really our best offer
    - Customer will challenge you, "For which side?"
    - If it is, don't fall into the trap of making revisions. If you make a revision once to your best price, what do you think will happen next time? It will turn out that your best price is just a starting price, right? If you want to sell your offer, don't use this expression unless it is really your fallback. Use for instance, "This is a fair offer." Bearing in mind current market conditions, you hope the buyer agrees to it but you still have some margin of maneuver just in case.

- What keeps you awake at night?:
    - This is sometimes used to find customer's real problems. Depending on the customer and your relationship with them you might get an honest answer, but be aware that not all buyers are that open or are in a mood to go into dissertations about their private life (sleep is their private terrain). They can simply say something like, "I sleep very well," or even, "My sleep is not your concern." Now what? Therefore, I recommend that you use this expression only when you have an already established relationship, otherwise use other approaches to find problem points.

- I need to ask my sales director/management if we can improve our offer.
    - Don't say this. It just discredits you in front of the customer. This makes it seem as if you're just a messenger without any decision-making capability. The next time the purchaser might well go directly to the sales director. Say instead, "Let me think about it, I'll see what I can do and I'll come back to you later." I've heard the expression, "I need to ask my sales director/management if we can improve our offer."

far too often, mainly from a junior sales rep. The intention is to save their image as the good guy (management are the bad ones) so if they can't improve the offer it's the management's fault. Well, as a sales rep you're the face of the company, for better or worse. Trying to save your face as the good guy will discredit you as professional. Being a good sales rep is not doing or saying yes to all that buyers ask. Be firm and consistent and you'll have their respect.

- This is a win/win situation
    - Use it with caution. Customers have also heard this too often. Save it and use it when for instance you've made concessions and expect them to do the same. If you use it before any concessions they will perceive it as you're winning and they are losing. Create an image of balance between your own and the customer's aims before you use this expression.
- **Let me talk about our Customer Value proposition:** This is when you think you come up with an offer that will get the customer hooked.
    - When you do this, be sure you know the customer very well and that you know their problems and value perception. You might risk the customer challenging you with the question, "Ok, so tell me everything about my company. How can you make a value proposition if you don't know what value means to us or where we could get value from a supplier perspective?"
- Special price for end of quarter or end of cycle period:
    - I recommend the use of any other reason for special prices. Campaigns, high stock levels, product rotation. If it becomes too obvious how regularly this is being done or that there's a specific periodicity, customers will plan accordingly and place their orders bearing

those periods in mind. So if the reason is less "timely" related, it's more difficult for the customer to play with it.

- **You're one of our strategic accounts.** You say this just to assure the customer that he's important and you won't treat him opportunistically.
    - The problem is that the customer won't feel flattered at all, they will instead expect special "treatment", special services and special prices. So be careful about how you use this expression. This is normally used when it's clear along the way that the customer is a Key Account - with their knowledge and intention as well – as a Key Account, management demands a particular approach and involvement of resources/time from both sides.

- **Bait and Switch:** You make a very attractive offer but later you change some premises that weren't clear at the beginning and assumed by the customer (with your knowledge):
    - Don't use this. It may get you one deal because the customer might be already trapped, but be assured that now the customer is lost – and he has also lost his credibility in you. This will work only for a one-shot deal and customer. Of course, you'll use all excuses and explanations that the customer wrongly assumed some detail as part of the deal, but remember what has been said earlier: clear communication is crucial in sales management.

- We don't name a price, we offer value.
    - This is a powerful one if used with caution and with the right customers. Let's face it, there are customers that are purely interested in the lowest price, particularly in the commodity business where service, delivery, quality or product performance are quite standard and easy to switch between different players. So it's

useless to talk about value and features or services to such a customer. But when addressed to the right account they will listen to your reasoning. Remember, very often buyers need your input and reasoning to explain internally their choices and deals.

- **Let me present you with our multiple-choice offer.** When you prepare an offer and give the customer the choice between A, B or C, each with different premises.
    - o My advice is, don't propose more than two, due to the high risk of getting things too complicated – for you and buyer- and lose the control. Another risk to bear in mind with this approach is that customers will start "playing" with them all, saying, "I want to offer A but with that part of B and that part of C." Set the rules clearly at the beginning. And always avoid having only one parameter changing between offers. If you have only one parameter in play, the customer will find out its cost or its numeric representation and will use it in future negotiations. When you have more than one parameter changing between two offers, it gets difficult for the customer to know the price or cost of each one, therefore will make him chose the offer that covers his critical needs.

        If you come up with two options, should you accept to merge or create a "hybrid" between them? Yes, as long as you properly manage the different premises of each and don't leave yourself exposed.

- Let's use the "card game" to find your priority needs.
    - o This is not so common, as its acceptance (by both sellers and buyers) has been quite low, but always good to be aware of. Mainly applied in complex negotiations or organizations when far too many parameters are pointed out by the seller as important, but the price is always the lowest possible. Sellers put down a few cards on the table with all kind of services

and options available and ask the buyer to pick up the three or five that are really important. Options are often, "Security of supply", "Price", "Quality", "Proximity", "Tech support" and so on. The purpose is to narrow down the customer's real needs, to segregate what they really need and what they thought they need but in the end, is not important. It's like selecting a "Must have", "Nice to have" and "Disposable". With this information, sellers can build up their offers in the most competitive manner, by taking out unnecessary services or features. Many customers don't like this kind of approach. The sales rep's intent is clear and noble: to know exactly what is important to the customer, but the "game" aspect of it tends to discourage customers to adhere. In that case, I'd rather have an open and honest discussion and use the "sensing questionnaire" to find out the customer's real needs and not the ones we think they have or even those *they* think they have.

- **We are market leaders**. This is commonly used in power-play discussions. To show strength and reassure customers, sales rep use it as a flag, so that customers feel proud or honored to do business with a leader.
    - Will it fly? Won't the customer instead feel doubtful and wondering how much more is he paying to work with a market leader? What are you giving or providing that others can't? What is the real benefit for the customer (in his eyes) of working with a market leader? Often this expression is perceived as arrogance, so if you use it, be clear about any benefit for the customer.
- Our product can help you reduce your costs.
    - Don't use this statement just because it sounds nice or there's a very small likelihood that is correct. Use

concrete data or facts that can easily be seen by the other side. Is your product increasing production rates? Reducing consumption? Replacing two or three different products? Delivered in different packaging and thus needing less manpower in the warehouse? Remember, customers listen to all these "clichés" every day. If you use them just as a "sounds nice cliché" it will be nothing more than an annoyance to the buyer. But if you back up your claim with facts, you'll stand out from your competitors. You won't be just a big mouth, you'll be the "go to" guy.

- **We're a customer-focused company.** This is one of the most often used sales sentences so it doesn't have any impact or persuasive power at all.
  - Are you doing what customers really need and want or are you just optimizing costs and providing what best suits your business model? What is your customer satisfaction rate (if you have any)? Can you sustain that with data and factual information? How's your quality control system? What did you implement or adapt following customer feedback? Customer focus should be at the heart of any business, though I regret to say this has become an empty slogan, an advert. Most of the time that expression has the opposite impact or just adds to customer bitterness. So don't use it at all, or use it with caution (when, for instance, you did follow a customer recommendation)

Main message wrap-up:

- Market is short
- This is a win/win situation
- Let me tell you about our value proposition
- Special price due to end of the quarter sales
- You're one of our strategic accounts
- Bait and switch
- I will present you a multiple choice offer
- We are market leaders
- We're a customer focused company

13

Frequently ASKED Questions:

What will B2B marketing and sales look like in the future?

Triggered by the explosion of the internet and the use of new technologies, there's a lot of noise and debate about the (so far) current sales channels and approaches. With the expansion of social selling, e-biz and AI, there's a certain apprehension that in the future we'll need fewer salespeople in the field and the B2B sales field model will be obsolete or old fashion.

Sure, the internet and technology are changing and molding all walks of life and business – examples like Uber, Airbnb, Amazon, or Alibaba – and surely these will impact the B2B marketing and sales processes. But to what extent? A real revolution or a simple shift?

The more conservative wing will say, B2B sales cycles and product cycles are much longer than B2C, therefore no such revolution will occur, rather remain as is and be boosted by new technologies. It won't mean a cut, but a reinforcement of the current sales process and field salespeople.

Fact is, No one knows.

No one knows. We might guess and believe from a number of studies or trends that it might be going this or that way, but *there is nothing that can be used with accuracy to predict what the future will bring.* This is scientifically proved and applies to Marketing as it applies to any other thing in life. It's very easy to look in the rearview mirror and explain what happened back there, it's not that easy to look through the windshield and predict the road ahead. Far too many things, events, and circumstances will jump in unexpectedly – so we never know where the road leads or which exit will we should take to on embark on a new journey. We will adapt, and yes, we should anticipate, but not because of any slight euphoria, but based on as many facts as possible, and some guts.

One side might argue **"But technology and trends have created a new way of marketing"**....yes, it's true. On the way, the messages are built and conveyed, on the tools and skills used. But marketing remains pretty much alive and growing every day. Did marketers disappear?

The other side will counter argue **"B2B has a longer sales cycle than B2C"** therefore no revolution will occur, there's a higher need for human interaction. Yes, there is. Let's be honest. *Already today, most of my work as a salesperson is done using remote tools (email, phone, telecoms, cloud systems, video calls with my customers on the other side of Europe, etc. etc.) and all this technology leads to speed and ease of contact and information sharing with impact on the field.*

Companies that used to have several sales reps in the field have reduced the numbers in many cases to a single sales rep per region or country.

Changes knocked on the door a while ago. We've seen companies "route to market" changing with the adoption of technology. We've seen a growing trend of teams as "telesales" or " home-based salespeople". So ignoring that technology has an impact on marketing and sales because the need for person-to-person contact is too naïve. Technology impacting B2B marketing and sales isn't the future, it's the present, or it's been ongoing for quite a while. Although it didn't kill existing sales models, it shaped them. Video and DVD's didn't kill the cinema. Sure, it was Impacted and had times of struggle, but it adapted, reshaped itself and today cinemas remain alive and kicking.

So what will be the future of marketing and sales in B2B?

An activity heavily based on cooperation, support, speed, access to data and market shifts supported by tailor-made solutions enhanced by technology will surely lead to an impact on the headcount. Not really a reduction but a selection. But, there's one common denominator: people will still be there, on one side and the other, at the heart of the B2B sales/purchase/marketing. And if you're skeptical about this or if you're fearing the technology will lead you to lose your job, remember, someone will be needed to sell that technology, so instead of resisting the imminent change, use it in your favor. Adapt. The ability to adapt to new environments is in every person's DNA. Resistance won't work.

As opposed to B2C (where with a click we can order a meal, shoes, gadgets or flowers) **B2B is pretty much based on completely different foundations:**

> The need for expertise, the need for market feedback, the need for interaction with someone who can provide you with more, much more than a price. In the B2B world, price is important, but there is much more to it than in the B2C world.
>
> So when you ask for feedback from a B2B customer who might have access to e-biz or online platforms to make some of his purchases, the answer is quite unanimous: "I can use the platforms but I need to talk to a salesperson to understand the background, the outlook and discuss options and negotiate prices." **That's also the base of B2B: negotiation, expertise, solutions, alternatives, advice, support and the list goes on.**
>
> There are certain items or services that can be done or acquired by using much more technology and with almost no human interaction: items that are easy to find, not important to your company and where quality of service is quite standard.
>
> In this case, the supplier is a vendor, like a vending machine - I need 100 pens, take this $10. That's it. Don't waste my time. **Would you have the same approach with feedstocks, raw materials, products**

or services that are crucial to your production or to your services? I wouldn't.

Huge developments have been made in terms of AI, AR, big data and other things once labeled as science fiction. All of them are a reality today, not some dream of the future. Instead of ignoring or fearing them, start adapting and embracing their eventual opportunities and anticipate their threats.

Why do Sales Directors set unrealistic targets?

Every year there's a wide range of salespeople whining about their targets, how unrealistic they are and the frustration it brings when they're chasing something that from the start, seems a lost race.

Well, there are three different sides to that story. Here are the most common ones:

1. **Scenario where you're told to "speak your mind" but in the end, management doesn't care about your arguments:**

Targets are set in a top-down mode from CEO/Management throughout the different layers of the organization, and at a certain point, they reach...the sales team. So your Sales Director doesn't have much of a choice other than to pass them on.

Eventually, he might challenge his reporting line – depending on his level of ambition and career growth – but he doesn't want to show a negative mindset and unwillingness to take challenges – even knowing the targets are out of reach and will lead to frustration– so he passes them on to the team.

So, during your target-setting meeting, you'll state that those targets are completely out of reach, but your Sales Director will tell you, "Yes, I understand your concerns but...." At this point, you should be aware that your argument won't change a thing. This is not a target agreement; it's a target setting. It's not about what you think, it's about what the company needs and your availability to support it. This might sound harsh, but that's what it is, regardless how much you'll moan about it.

2. **Scenario aiming to challenge the sales team out of their comfort zones. As opposed to the first scenario, there's open discussion and sharing of the vision.**

If you don't stretch people, they will never know their potential. If you set achievable goals, where is the challenge for your team? If you can get 100 why can't you get 110? Setting challenging targets is – depending on how the message and vision are conveyed – an excellent strategy to push people out of their comfort zone. If a project is deemed to be finished in six months, why can't it be done in four? Yes, you'll need a few adjustments, shift prioritization, delegate more and cut some downtime. But what if it's worth the effort and that is perfectly clear for everyone?

3. **Scenario where salespeople are on autopilot and don't like their world to be shaken. They know best their region/country and feel that any target above "conservative" is unrealistic:**

Very often salespeople fight or hope to get a "comfortable" target and see anything over their expectations, as "unrealistic". Well, believe me, I've seen many unrealistic targets being met and exceeded, how can that be?

For a sales rep, a good target is the one he sees as realistic. But where is the challenge in this case? What's the point of chasing something that from the beginning you know is within reach? Shouldn't you aim for the extra mile? The cherry on top of the cake?

I do understand that if presented in "cold blood", some targets might seem unrealistic and lead to team frustration and even cut the motivation of the individuals.

The key here is, the ability of management and the Sales Director to sustain those numbers with accurate foundations, with a vision of the how, who, what, when and why it's possible to reach them. The role of the sales team is to be open, expectant, willing and believing the story they've been told. If you set targets without a proper story behind them and have a sales team on "autopilot" mode, the targets will indeed seem unrealistic. Because there's a lack of background (Management) and lack of belief and resistance to change (Sales team).

One aspect that plays a major role in all these discussions is the rewarding or bonus schemes. Companies have different compensation plans and bonus layers. If those aren't very clear on their fundamentals and accountability, they might impact the level of commitment (up or down) of a sales team. If within the metrics of bonuses are parameters completely out of the sales executive activity, it can undermine ambition and effort.

How to handle objections in sales?

With gratitude.

There's a very well-known motto in sales.

"If they accepted my proposal without any objection, I was too cheap".

It's in the purchaser's DNA to object. Now, that can be done at completely different levels or arguments (valid or not) and might require different approaches. However, there's at least one common thing to bear in mind: the need for active listening and understanding of the customer's objection **(is this a real objection or a simple negotiation trick?)** – to know if what he tells you is really a concern or regardless of what he tells you, what he expects is a price revision.

Listen. Don't rush to answer on the spot. Don't put yourself immediately in a defense or response mode. Hold your horses. Listen to him, watch him, and ask more details about his rejection. Quality issue? At what level? Specification? Processing formula? Machinery regulation?

Use one of the most successful "lean" approaches: the "five why" question. For each layer go deeper, don't let him just wave some purchaser cliché at you.

Let him talk. What is he objecting about? Focus on his arguments, not on him as a person. This is not an arm wrestling fight. This is positioning – and how can you bridge your arguments with his objections? Very often people get emotional with objections (or rejections) and lose the direction of the negotiation, to a point that the opportunity is lost as their egos got in the way.

It's not about you being right and him being wrong. It's not about what you want. First and foremost is what he wants/needs. Listen to him and take it from there. Often they have gaps and holes in their own objections. When you show real interest or try to uncover their objection they provide you with info they wouldn't otherwise. Often they're just testing the waters (and why shouldn't they?) to see how far you would go or how tough you are.

But bear in mind that often they are right. You're on "autopilot" and you didn't notice that your proposal didn't meet their real needs (but *yours*) and that technically, there's not a good fit. That quality-wise it's not what they need, therefore you should have involved your technical or quality people. That they are on a different quality level than the standard customer or need some additional feature that you simply forgot.

That's why it's so important to listen and be genuinely grateful or open to discussing the objections.

Another good reason to be grateful for genuine objections is because customer objections are the best feedback you could have, and it's a great improvement opportunity. For your company, for your product, for your services, for your package or for yourself, as a salesperson, for your negotiation skills. It's a unique chance to pick up a "fight" in a constructive manner, if it's not a solely a negotiation objection, it's selling. Overcoming obstacles.

Don't let a "no" blind you or your ego. Pick it up and turn it into a yes. That's what great salespeople do.

But also bear in mind the following:

- Is it worth the time/effort dedicated to that customer?
- Do you perceive that the objection is vague and nonsense?

- Does the customer or prospect really need your product and is he willing to value it if the objection is properly handled?

If the answer is no, thank them for their time, keep the door open but focus on your potential customers, not on those who systematically use you to benchmark.

It's useless to deal with the objections of customers you don't want, need or fit your business.

Just as a recap, these are the most common sales objections:

- Price too expensive
- We have sufficient suppliers
- We don't need your product/service
- Budget restraints
- I can't decide, need to consult someone
- Wrong timing
- We have no interest in your product/service
- I'll think about it

How can I be best in class as a sales manager

You'll probably be expecting a process or a step-by-step system. There certainly are a good number of tools, processes, approaches, and methods that every sales manager should be aware and use, but there's not one where you'll stand out. There's no handbook telling you how to become a pro sales executive. There's just field work, learning, and growth.

Nowadays anyone can have access to and acquire skills or knowledge. But not everyone will reach a top level in sales. Because the secret isn't in following a step by step process, but in the individuals themselves.

Sales is about a mix of things and one important part of it is who you are vs who the purchaser is. Processes, methods, and systems are just means that will complete the puzzle.

So instead of focusing on systems and methods (you can do that at any time and anywhere) focus on this:

Empathy, persuasion, and capacity to build trust and long-term relationships. Technology can enable and speed up processes, but people are at the heart of anything being transmitted from A to B in the corporate world.

Don't look at customers as numbers. Customers aren't an abstract thing. It's all about people. People who have personal lives, good and bad days as you do. Individuals with ups and downs, with ambitions and setbacks, with wants and needs, with limited time available.

Bearing that in mind, the best way to build rapport is by showing genuine interest in individuals (or corporations as their representatives), their wants and needs.

Would selling a fridge to an Eskimo make you a greater or better salesman? No. It would certainly make you earn some bucks and the admiration of a short-sighted manager, but wouldn't serve any purpose in the mid/long term.

Build and maintain relationships (internally and with customers) in a very respectful manner.

Build customer relationships based on trust and sincerity.

Work on long-term relationships, balanced with exploring short-term opportunities or margin optimizations.

As I said in an earlier chapter, you'll need to master these attributes:

- Empathy: Ability to understand and share the feelings of another
- Persuasion: Action aimed to change a person's attitude or behavior
- Influence: The action of producing effects on the actions, behavior or opinions of another
- Capacity to build trust and long-term relationships.

- Clear communication
- Active listening
- Be passionate
- Learn. Learn from others
- Don't sell. Become a source: a trusted source and resource.

Should healthy competition among sales team be promoted?

This is always a temptation and a tricky position to be in from the sales director side, as he will often be challenged on this point by higher management.

My personal feeling is, it's not competing with my peers that will motivate me or improve my commitment and achieve results. Best practices though, are always welcome and should always be shared amongst the team.

To be very honest, my experience with regards to competitions amongst peers has the reverse result. That label of "healthy competition" has always, in the vast majority of people, shown a negative connotation or the opposite of what "healthy" should mean.

Speaking of team cohesion, the less harmful approach I've seen so far is the establishment of very clear rewards and incentives. Transparency of bonus schemes (that are less and less transparent or with metrics that are out of the sales rep's control), career evolution, recognition and praise from a higher level.

Unfortunately, in most companies I've been involved with, and others I know personally, this process is very opaque, and staff have the feeling that the opacity is there on purpose.

In a team competition "model", rating a team member with the highest grade means you'll need to find a victim to "downgrade" even if he isn't that bad, but you need to reach the overall target and it must end equal to 100. This is a nonsense, as the performance appraisal is conditioned from the beginning and won't be a fair ranking on performance but to meet the company's process or guideline.

With all that said, it depends a lot on the kind of business, the teams, and market approach. For instance, a team operating in EU with a sales rep per country. The southern guys will argue that the economics and market are far more favorable in the northern countries. That's a fact. But at the same time, there's no ideal world. What you can do here is have specific targets that are in line with market realities (for instance different metrics). Difficult, but not impossible.

I would say that in order to avoid damaging the team spirit with a team ranking, you can create a kind of team target besides the individual targets. You can argue, "There will always be those who contribute and those who collect same rewards." That's a different story.

Underperformance remains a kind of taboo in most companies. It's one thing to get below target due to some very concrete and factual circumstances, while another is to simply lag behind, moaning and complaining about the market circumstances.

We need also to have in mind the "soft skills" factors, that can't be measured with standard metrics but are equally important for the business, something you can't see in end numbers but observe from a sales rep's behaviour: team player, attitude, commitment, sharing knowledge and best practices, respectful behaviour. The lack of those behaviors should be penalized so as not to hurt the spirit of the team.

Healthy competition inside a team may be well-intended, but I've often seen sales colleagues overruling common sense and good working practices just for the sake of higher numbers. Don't forget, numbers can be creative. I've been in a team of ten in a major oil and chemical company, most of them good folks and professional but at a certain moment the moral went down tremendously because our commercial director had the brilliant idea of a "healthy competition" within the team.

The reason? One or two weren't playing by the rules, just to reach outstanding numbers and visibility. It is discouraging and unfair when you work in a professional and responsible manner and see someone showing off when you know the practices are at least, doubtful.

Think long term, don't try to invent shortcuts. Shortcuts may bring short-term gains but will also bring long-term pains.

Before embracing the healthy competition approach, ask yourself:

- Do I have the right team?
    - Are they equality passionate, motivated, and equipped?
- Does competition amongst them improve them and their achievements – and what are the risks?
- What other approaches should I consider? (Training, shift regions/portfolios, projects, etc)

My motto is, as a team member, "You shouldn't compete with your peers, and you should *complete your peers and the business*."

In a cold call, how can I reach a decision-maker when I have a gatekeeper between us?

There isn't a single straight line, as it will always depend on:

a. Who is calling - personality, attitude, and behavior

b. Who is the gatekeeper (same as above)

c. The relevance of your product/service for them

d. Their kind of organization and purchasing department

e. Your voice. Tone, tune, and pace.

Probably in ten different attempts, you'll be able to get through in a few of them, but mostly you won't. That's the beauty of human interaction, it's not about an algorithm or process you can follow as a "step-by-step" guide, but about empathy, momentum, and some random parameters you can't figure out as they're changing each time you call.

Following the timeless motto, "Failing to prepare is preparing to fail." The better you're "equipped" the higher your chances will be:

- You don't know the decision maker's name/position?

    o Do your homework. Without that info, your chances are pretty low. How can you get it?

    o Through the GK. Have a well-rehearsed, polite and short pitch to tell him/her who'd you like to talk to and ask if he/she can put you through or provide a direct contact number so you can call later.

    o From folks in any other department (technical guys, for instance). They used to be pretty naïve in that sense, as their mindset is technical and they can tell you who the guy in charge is (or will tell it to your technical colleague).

    o The best and easiest is probably to search LinkedIn. Search by company, position, other colleagues' names etc. etc.

    o Another option is to search online corporate reports, as they often have that kind of information.

    o Last but not least, if possible, visit the company and inform the person at the reception desk that you're short on time but will need to talk to the purchaser later but you forgot his name/phone.

- Do you know the decision maker's name and position?

    This gives you a clear advantage.

    o When you call saying you want to talk to Mr. X in the purchasing department, the GK/receptionists just asks your name/company and puts you through. They don't ask or wonder if you're a new guy trying to make contact or if you're already in discussions with the purchaser.

    o The purchaser doesn't recognize you and ask the GK to

tell you he's not available? Here you have a good chance to get his email. Tell the GK you forgot his email and she'll give it without a second thought.

- o Despite knowing the purchaser's name, the GK keeps blocking you, asking the purpose of the call and a few other questions? Tell her it's to follow up on a previous discussion you had with him. Don't worry, he won't remember.

How can a sales director make his salespeople more productive?

Keep them happy. You can see some statistics in the below snapshot:

Happy people produce **37% Higher sales**

Happy people are **31% more productive**

Happy people have **3X The creativity**

Happy people pull out the stops and have **19% Higher Task accuracy**

Source: mumfordsole LLC

But how do you do that?

- Let them make their work, don't flood them with systems, tools and processes to which they don't see the benefit nor has its purpose been explained. Keep them happy.

I've worked for a major oil/chemical company where we were very frustrated and lacked motivation because of so much bureaucracy, that once we decided to make a study on how much time we had left to be used with our customers.

An astonishing 65% of the time was used for purely internal purposes: meetings, systems, and processes to fill in every day, databases to update regularly, conference calls, sales meetings, development programs, monthly discussions with the sales director, weekly team meetings, projects, updates of all matters – and the list would go on.

Try to visualize a sales team, where only 35% of their time was dedicated to their portfolio, to their clients. And we're not talking about any startup or an inexperienced company, but a big multinational in the world top ten ranking.

Based on my frustrations and experience, do you want to know how to motivate your salespeople?

Empower them: That's the best thing you can do with salespeople.

Make them accountable/responsible: People who feel responsible give back much more than you ask.

Take away or try to ease their frustrations.

Of course, they will always have to fill in forms and update databases, but please ensure they understand and see the benefits, for them, the team or the organization. Don't force them to do any tasks or routines they don't see any benefit in. Salespeople hate "tick the box" exercises, they're practical people, not bureaucrats.

You don't know their frustrations? Ask them. Openly.

What will make them more productive isn't a higher bonus but the smoothness and efficiency of their work.

Align your company and departments on the vision and targets. Very often salespeople have to "negotiate" or deal with more challenges internally than with their own customers. Crazy, yes? But reality.

Functions like credit, logistics, customer service, quality, production, and so on are often perceived as obstacles in the sales manager's life. It's not true, as they exist to support each other. But the gap is the message and the alignment in terms of KPI's and objectives (sometimes in conflict). Each department needs to understand each others roles and hurdles in order to better understand the business from an end to end perspective, but often companies work in small silos.

Get the optimal balance and cooperation between functions and departments and you'll get a more productive sales team.

- **Defend them, support them, protect them. Be their general. I'll do the max for anyone who's being there for me. Wouldn't you?**

Remember, whilst physical work is often expected to be rewarded with money, intellectual work is often expected to be rewarded with praise and recognition.

Will technology and the internet replace field salespeople?

The internet and F2F sales aren't competing with each other. They complement each other. Technology in itself isn't a long-term business but a business enabler and enhancer, always with people in between, in the frontline or in the background. Take the human factor out, and the business model will be gone.

You will be able to do quite a lot "virtually". At one of the major oil companies I've worked for, there has been a pilot program for more than 10 years to create a sales team called "telesales". People who wouldn't need to travel and would be doing sales from a hub using email, phone, video calls and so on. It was a B2B, commodity business, not some small item product, service or gadgets.

The objective was to handle the small and non-core accounts and optimizing resources/cutting costs, of course. Nothing is ever done for the sake of the customers. Even if they tell you otherwise. First and most important step in any project is always "how much will we earn/how much will we save?".

- All medium big and strategic accounts were still handled by Field based Account Managers.

As the term "telesales" was a bit detractive, after a few years they decided to rebrand it to "Office-Based Account Managers" allowing the team members to visit the customers once in a while for relationship building and long-term vision, or to explore potential.

I guess this last step was the right one in the right direction. But again, the scope was to keep this "lean and low-cost model" for non-core and non-strategic accounts in a mature and well-established brand in an established market managing existing portfolios.

A smaller team of Field Based Account Managers still existed but handling those strategic partners. As a big chunk of their portfolio had shifted to office-based people, they had fewer accounts to follow, therefore could dedicate more time and energy to exploring the full potential of the big sharks. That's how the company balanced the customer size portfolio, from the opportunistic and on/off customers to the strategic accounts, keeping a good balance in terms of revenues, options, and resources.

So my view is that with technology we'll definitely have fewer field sales reps, but relationship building, market expertise and strategic sourcing can't be done any other way than with human interaction and F2F meetings. Very simply put, what makes a great company isn't great product or services, but great people. A great product without a great sales team won't go far, while an average product with a great sales team can go far.

How can I find new clients?

Let's make this exercise as realistic as possible. It's not about "how a B2B company finds clients" but "Your B2B company finds clients". So, from the general to the specific. There are a lot of tools and systems, a lot of social media engagement programs and new technology strategies, but most of those will work well for some kind of companies/markets and will be less successful for others.

It would be completely useless for a company to invest time, resources and systems that aren't appropriate for their business model or sector. This is not "one size fits all" or "this is trending, let's use it".

You need to nail it down to the bone when we talk of very concrete industry segments or products, and furthermore, how each company deals with it. This is my personal experience and how I managed to find customers for the companies I've worked in for the last 15 years, and the approach many B2B are still applying. An important note is, this is mainly in the B2B commodities world. Products that in general, are an important part of the customer end products.

- Competitors of current customers – This is an excellent source, whether we get it directly from the customers or from other sources. Competitors of our customers are our ideal customer. They're in the same market, dynamics, processes, approvals, production processes, and so on. Imagine the time and energy you save by instead of searching around and qualifying leads you have them handed to you by your customers.

- Dormant or old customers – Another good source. Very often customers were left aside due to some dispute with the sales rep or a particular transaction. But be watchful – it can also be that they have been dropped due to bad credit line/performance at the time, or they were too small. Get in touch. Check their evolution and where they stand today.

- Trade fairs and expositions – Great and wide source when it's about a big or prestigious event in the industry. Besides a large number of potential customer that you can add to your list, you actually have the chance to meet and distribute your business card. Often, purchasers aren't there, but the attendees will give you the names of purchasers or other important stakeholders. Be aware though, that often you'll find a very wide scale of product users, from the one-time user to your ideal customer, so don't assume they're all good fishes for your net. You'll need to throw most of them out.

- Industry Associations – Also a good source of the main players in a certain sector.

- LinkedIn – Very useful and important to get leads and names of responsible people in each department (purchasing, marketing etc.)

Explore those above and measure each of them in terms of finding and perhaps actually capturing and attracting leads and prospects.

I remember once a big oil and chemical company I worked for outsourced a consultancy firm to find us some leads. In a first step, they sent us thousands of names. Guess what, indeed the names were using our products or in the same industry, but whilst our business was selling products in huge bulk quantities, 95% of those leads were buying a few cans a year. 4% of the names were already customers or names that we knew.

So it's a jungle out there, and people can become very excited by numbers that show up in a first research, but be aware to adjust your filters and criteria correctly, otherwise, the exercise will take much more time, energy and resources than the value it will bring. That's why it's important to try one system at a time and analyze the first results to see where it leads and if it's worth exploring further or move to another system.

What's the number of follow-ups before I get the sale?

For sure you've heard the statistics, or that it's common to say X or Z times, but you know what? Forget those statistics. They don't tell you anything at all, how they've been made up or what sources, scope, methods or input were used. They are too generic, too vague to be taken as a serious reference for your specific business.

The sale will depend on quite a few factors, but won't happen just because you're on the fourth follow-up, and according to the statistics, it's very likely to happen on the fifth. If you did your homework properly and created the right circumstances, it *can* happen by the fifth, but if you're just rolling and hoping the customer gets tired and says yes, it might well be that the customer is rolling and expecting that sooner or later you'll give up and stop annoying him.

Do you think the buyer will tell himself: "Ok, these people already did four follow-ups, now I have to buy!" Where's the science behind that?

With all that said, let's imagine you have six potential customers you've already been talking to for a while. Let's imagine you started the discussions or interactions all at the same time. Will they all buy after the same number of follow-ups? Of course not. Each has their own agenda, priorities, and urgencies to deal with purchasing. They're not following your agenda, they're following their agenda and their move will not depend on your product, your timing, your approach, or your arguments, but on how much all of that fits with their situation and momentum.

And you can argue – but what if I dedicated the same attention and time to each, provided requested info and clarified all questions to all of them at the same time, why don't they buy around the same period or after the same number of follow up's? For the reasons I pointed out before, plus the fact that you've not been listening or have been attentive enough. It's not about your agenda, which is what you want, it's about their agenda.

Because it's not about you, what you want and what you expect from them. It's about them. What they want, what they need and what they expect from you.

Remember a very common saying in the sales world, "When you have what the other guy wants, you have a deal."

Therefore, the number of follow-ups will depend on how much "to the point" information you can tackle from the buyers perspective and need, not from your perspective, on each round, and how deeply you're able to dig into the customer's real needs in each round. If you don't go deep and discover what really drives the customer and what really stands in between you. It might take a long time (more than eight follow-ups) before you're able to connect and to openly tackle the customer's real needs with trust and a long-term view. If you can do this you might have a deal after the fourth round.

The important thing is not the number of follow-ups, but your ability to sense the customer's main points or interests and be able to present your product/service as a solution to them.

How is it a typical day for a sales manager?

As you can imagine, sales management roles aren't always based on routines, and of course, there is a variety of tasks or duties you need to fulfill. Sometimes not in a day, but in a week or in a month. I'll try anyway to share a picture of what an average day of work is like, but this is something you can't always stick to. Companies, sales directors, and regions might ask for different setups.

Also bear in mind that most sales managers are working from a home office base. Sometimes they will visit their company offices but most of the time, if they're not traveling, they catch up with their lives and work from home.

One of the reasons is, they are "field-based" so they cover a whole region, country or industry segment. So they might live closer to those markets instead of their company office.

So a "standard" working day of mine can be as follows:

1. Get up to speed – information and checking where I stand

   - Check my agenda and upcoming teleconferences and meetings and also check on the following days
   - Check my "to-do tasks" or pending actions and define prioritizations of the day
   - Check inbox and tackle incoming emails also by the level of urgency plus relevance.
   - Check where do I stand with my monthly sales
   - List of customers lagging behind to take action
   - Check how feedstocks are evolving
   - Check how prices are going and the market index

2. Creative work: Action based on info gathered and plan for the month by means of email, telephone or preparing a visit:

   - Tackle urgent/important pending topics/emails

- Tackle follow up on leads or opportunities
- Plan + action for underperforming accounts
- Call customers, discuss market in general and share your price intentions
- Call colleagues to see how they see their market and competition behavior.
- Work on any ongoing project (presentation)
- Work on overdue

3. Managerial work: Routine tasks, pending topics (not so urgent but important), admin work, bureaucracy:

- Work on issues such as logistics, claims, approvals
- Prepare expenses tickets and report
- Insert customer prices into the system
- Send confirmation price emails to customers
- Answer customer center requests or queries
- Plan visits
    - Combine more than one customer around the same region
    - Check distances, flights, car traveling
    - Take care of bookings and block your calendar to avoid conflicts.
- If visiting with a colleague, ensure the calendar and trip options work for all (your side + customer side)
- Work on lead generation
- Plan your following day, have it visualized in your mind and note down the prioritization

Of course, this is a draft for whenever I'm working in the home office

– when I'm traveling most of the above remains on hold. Often I do some "managerial work" in the evenings or I'll have to catch up on my return.

Here are a couple of other responsibilities that have some kind of periodicity:

Weekly:

- Overdue report: list to act on overdue accounts
- Talk to your sales director about how things are going

Bi-Weekly:

- Team teleconference
- Management/sales team/pricing/market feedback/teleconference

Monthly:

- Sales forecast for the next month
- Filling and sending the expense report (I usually don't let it pile up, and prepare it throughout the month)
- All prices must be in the system (again, also doing it throughout the month)

Randomly:

- Contract preparation, approvals, and updates in the system
- Rebate accruals confirmations
- Complaint reports outcome to be shared/discussed with customers
- Attending training/development
- Attending sales team meeting with management
- Giving a presentation, sharing best practices, coaching inside sales

Any tips on traveling preparations?

Advice I can share with those thinking about taking a new job that requires a lot of international travel

Travelling for fun once in a while is one thing, traveling regularly for work is another. In the latter, you have specific goals and objectives for your trip and you need to prepare for meetings and map out how to most effectively manage each business day in order to avoid a mountain of things to do when you come back home.

To help make your upcoming business trip a smooth one, I first recommend that you clean up your email or chat messages backlog.

Second, document all of the following information in your calendaring tool:

- Meeting days and times - start times, estimated duration
- Meeting locations, distance, method of transportation, route and estimated transit times.

Lastly, consider the impact your trip can have on your personal life. If you're single or an empty nester you may love the lifestyle, but if you're recently married or have small kids, frequent business travel could take a toll. If you fall into the second category, I recommend discussing things with your wife/kids in a realistic way. Don't be afraid to discuss the negative possible impacts the travel could have on everyone, not just yourself. I've seen a number of colleagues end up on their own because they didn't have realistic conversations and notions about the impact this could have on their lives.

What is different about business in the countries you work in vs. where you live? How can business professionals from both countries reach common ground?

There are two things I'd recommend for you keep in mind about international business travel:

Cultural awareness. Try to keep a good mindset on the importance of diversity and inclusiveness. Keep an open mind and be ready to adapt, not only the way you come across to others but the way you develop your business proposal and the way you try to close a business deal. Reset your expectations when needed.

Why is this important?

Every country, even sometimes every region, has specific etiquette you should be aware of. For example, the Dutch are very direct and looking to quickly accomplish a goal or get to an agreement. On the flipside, Nordics are calculative and factual. And South European people bring a more emotional aspect to business. They also don't mind taking their time to make important business decisions.

Lastly, in some Asian cultures, as a matter of respect, they don't like to formally tell you "no" to your face. You might be excited because you initially get cues associated with a "yes." For example, you may receive a smile from a potential customer after you've presented your business offer, therefore you may assume that you'll soon close the deal. However, weeks later you find out that the customer was never actually interested.

In all of these scenarios, the question to ask yourself is, "How can we best cooperate?"

1. Etiquette

    Make sure to study the culture and business etiquette for the country you plan to visit. If you don't have colleagues in the country you're traveling to, look for information and advice online. Popular information to note would include: habits, business culture, climate, gifting etiquette and common work schedules (office hours, the timing of lunches, dinners, happy hours and which you might be expected to participate in with clients, colleagues, etc.). For engaging conversations, it's best to stay up-to-date on local news.

Best international travel tips

Here's what has helped me avoid surprises or forgetting key items:

1. Prior to the trip, double check that you have the hotel addresses, customer addresses, booking confirmations and phone numbers.

2. Do a quick mental walkthrough of your agenda for each day of the trip
3. Pack in advance. And if you can't, at least build a pile of essentials in a single place, so as not to forget anything.
4. Check currency, passports, and visas (if applicable)
5. Check in online in advance
6. On the day of departure, arrive at the airport with ample time to spare. If you don't, you're at risk of missing flights/connections and/or experiencing flight overbooking.

Remember, you're not a judge, jury or master of the truth. Observe, understand, absorb, respect.

Don't expect to have your usual comforts. (Example: a particular food, beer or Starbucks). Be open, be bold, be accepting in your attitude.

One last piece of advice, don't post photos of your downtime to Facebook or other social media during your business trip (at least not of yourself having great fun). Even if it was a well-deserved break and in line with business principles, it might not be well perceived by management, colleagues or future employers.

Can a sales executive excel in any market segment?

Any market or industry segment will have its own dynamics, and you need to be able to mold yourself into the reality of your field.

Just as an example, if you come from a commodity business and are starting a position in Specialties, this will require a shift and readiness for several changes. Be prepared for different selling cycles, much longer approval processes, much longer on-boarding process of new customers, and different pricing approaches. Commodity products are a bit market-driven, specialties are almost "tailor-made solutions" with a completely different pricing setup.

It will be quite different selling products versus selling services. Moving from one to the other will require a step back and an analysis of the main market drivers and specifics of the business from the different angles. Of course, the basic pillars will be the same (empathy, trust, etc) but you need to be ready to speed up or slow down in a couple of other areas (closing the deals faster, adding features, getting technical support, bigger or smaller turnovers etc).

Will someone who has been extremely good at selling product commodities be good at selling services? Most likely yes, but will need a period of adaptation to embed into the new environment and adjust his skills/priorities accordingly.

Is it the same, selling to dedicated purchasers vs functions?

Probably not, you may face different challenges.

Purchasers, as described earlier, are somehow quite predictable, or tend to follow certain patterns. If you need to sell a product or service to any department where your counterpart isn't a purchaser, but the department manager, it might get a bit tricky. As they are not "professional buyers" they might surprise you with questions, demands or challenges you were not expecting. Imagine you're selling software to the HR department. They will look at the tool mainly from an HR perspective, functionality and cost. Even if you proudly bring along many other features hoping they add value to your offer you might be disappointed as they may not consider them to be of any benefit. So always bear in mind who your counterpart is and try to meet their expectations from their angle as closely as possible. They will not follow the "purchasing path". They have a need, they have a budget, they will have several options. You will tell me, "That's what purchasers have." No, purchasers go much further and will use many other purchasing techniques. Does this make it easier to sell to functions? No, not really. Remember, with purchasers you build a relationship, with functions most of the time will be a very occasional sale and probably not recurrent, so you don't have many chances to win the next time.

Does selling relatively high-cost items require the same skills as selling relatively low-cost or cheap products?

As you could see in previous sections, customers will rank and dedicate time/money on their purchasing according to the level of relevance of the items they buy.

So if your item is low relevant on their end and easy to find, you can expect they will dedicate less time and will put quite some pressure on pricing. So you need to adjust your strategy as per the purchaser's strategic intent. Don't waste time with complex offers and stories as they won't be needed or appreciated by the seller. Keep it as lean, simple and competitive as possible.

On the other hand, if you're selling products that are relevant to them, you'll notice they dedicate time to listen, talk, discuss and negotiate. Which one is harder? Difficult to say as it depends on how do you look at "hard". Selling relevant items will require more market background, negotiation and persuasion skills. Low-cost items will demand resilience, patience, and frequent acceptance of "no's". At the same time, it will be less painful to lose a deal or a customer.

SUPPORT MATERIAL

You can follow or connect with Amaro Araujo in social media:

Twitter: @AmaroAlive

Linkedin: https://www.linkedin.com/in/amaroaraujo/

his personal blog at: **amaroaraujo.com**

In his personal blog, you'll get access to the support templates and drafts mentioned in his book.

You can also check his other books or online courses.

ABOUT THE AUTHOR

Amaro Araujo is a Portuguese citizen married to Margarida Araujo with whom they have two kids (grown-up by now) Igor and Debora.

Living in the Netherlands since 2007 he speaks six languages and works as an international sales executive handling strategic accounts.

He's passionate about life, has an inquisitive mind, is a daydreamer and writer.

He loves sports, and exercises on a very regular basis. Reading and writing are some of his passions, together with watching a good movie or TV series. Cooking for the family and friends is precious to him.

Walking enjoying nature is something he does on a daily basis as practice of the art of standing still and disconnecting from the noise and rush of today, that in most cases leads nowhere.

In international sales for more than 20 years, he has beaten targets across different businesses, handled the most complex accounts, negotiated with the most challenging customers, landed multiple multi-million-dollar deals and beaten the most challenging targets.

www.ingramcontent.com/pod-product-compliance
Lightning Source LLC
Chambersburg PA
CBHW070251230526
45470CB00002B/568